LISTENING TO THE CHURCH

LISTENING TO THE CHURCH

A Realistic Profile
of Grass Roots Opinion

Virgil Wesley Sexton

Abingdon Press

Nashville New York

LISTENING TO THE CHURCH

Copyright © 1971 by Abingdon Press

ISBN   0-687-22123-4

Library of Congress Catalog Card Number: 73-162455

SET UP, PRINTED, AND BOUND BY THE
PARTHENON   PRESS,   AT   NASHVILLE,
TENNESSEE, UNITED STATES OF AMERICA

To my wife, Catherine
who is also worth listening to

ACKNOWLEDGMENTS

The author wishes to express appreciation to the many whose contributions, direct or indirect, helped to shape this book; but he is particularly indebted to the following:

Dr. Gerald L. Clapsaddle, who heads United Methodism's Division of Coordination, Research, and Planning and who enthusiastically supports the planning process of which this book is a part;

Dr. Alan K. Waltz and Dr. Ernest T. Dixon, Jr., staff colleagues, for valued counsel and encouragement;

The program council staffs of the denominational annual conferences and the general agency staff for stimulating participation in sharing attitudes; and

Many thousands of United Methodists and other people in the fifty states who shared their feelings and attitudes about the church and the world.

FOREWORD

The well-documented material in this significant volume is a message to the church from its basic constituency. In the past the strong forward movements in the church have emerged largely from the councils and general boards. The "handed down" concept of emphases and programs is not a myth. Most of the advances in the church have traveled that route.

Dr. Virgil Sexton, working through the Section of Planning, a major structure within the Program Council of The United Methodist Church, has prepared for a fresh and creative advance for the church in mission by reversing this process. In this day the search for goals, priorities, and methods has begun at the grass roots. Out in the field where the issues are known, where the people are, and where the power for change lies, a process has emerged that will move up through the church to carry it forward significantly in the middle years of the 70s.

In this volume the reader will observe the results of what is probably the most thorough, comprehensive, and inclusive survey in the history of the church. Literally thousands of persons in the church's constituency in every segment of its presence across the nation have been involved in the planning process reflected in the following pages. In this study the grass roots have been reliably heard from and a plan for action has "come up" rather than being "handed down." It is this inclusive process that makes this volume worthy of the study of all in the church.

The research and evaluation of findings presented in the following pages have been well done. The planning process has been forcefully executed and reported in a style that will hold the reader's interest. The task remains for the church to measure up to the rising expectations of its constituency and capture new ground for Christ in the church.

W. Ralph Ward, Jr.
Bishop, Syracuse Area
President, Program Council
The United Methodist Church

CONTENTS

CONTENTS

1

AN EAR TO THE GROUND

> And the Church must be forever building, and always
> decaying, and always being restored. . . .
> And all that is ill you may repair if you walk together
> in humble repentance. . . .
> And all that was good you must fight to keep with
> hearts as devoted as those of your fathers who
> fought to gain it.
> —T. S. Eliot, "Choruses from 'The Rock' "

What do you suppose the members of a major Protestant denomination would say that their church priorities ought to be in the 1970s? Would there be wide divisions of opinion? Would sectionalism be apparent? Would the national church leadership be in sharp disagreement with the average church member?

One such denomination, The United Methodist Church, is systematically looking for answers. At last report, all Methodists, of which United Methodists are the major part, were described as:

14 percent of the national population

54 percent female

91 percent white

20 percent college, 54 percent high school, and 26 percent grade school in educational level

36 percent manual laborers, 24 percent professionals, 21 percent nonlaborers, 11 percent white-collar workers, and 8 percent farm workers by employment

45 percent fifty years of age or older, 37 percent thirty to forty-nine, and 16 percent twenty-one to twenty-nine

40 percent Democratic, 34 percent Republican, and 24 percent Independent in avowed political affiliation

35 percent living in rural areas, 22 percent in cities of fifty to five hundred thousand, 21 percent in cities larger than that, and 19 percent in towns of twenty-five hundred to fifty thousand

30 percent midwestern, 30 percent southern, 23 percent eastern, and 17 percent western in national membership

35 percent weekly worshipers as compared to the national average of 43 percent.[1]

From this widely varied membership, answers have begun to emerge. Interestingly, there are apparently no radical differences of opinion between denominational leadership and the average church member in their view of priorities. There are indications, however, of disagreement about how to act on those priorities.

Nor are sharp sectional differences apparent; in fact, an astonishing agreement is found throughout the denomination.

The basis of these statements is an analysis of a nationwide denominational response to an invitation to express attitudes. The invitation was issued as a part of a planning process being followed by the United Methodist general Program Council.

This national body of the denomination was mandated by the General Conference, United Methodism's highest legislative body, to study the need for any special emphasis in the church for the years 1972 through 1976.[2] In order to avoid a bureaucratic, handed-down answer to that mandate, wide participation in its design was invited.

The invitation went out through several channels. First, a tear sheet was placed in a denominational monthly magazine,

---

[1] Gallup Opinion Index, Special Report on Religion by George H. Gallup, Jr. and John O. Davies III, February, 1969, p. 29.

[2] See *The Book of Discipline of The United Methodist Church*, 1968 (Nashville: The Methodist Publishing House), p. 207.

The Interpreter. The ten local church leaders in each parish who receive the magazine were invited to express themselves about general trends, sharp issues, and church needs as they saw them for the 70s. Over two thousand have so far replied. Every mail brings more. Most are accompanied by pages of written comments.

In addition, a larger field instrument was designed with the advice of leaders from local areas who were to use it. Early in that discussion these leaders rejected a simple instrument. "If you use this," they said, "you can expect mostly pious platitudes in response." As a result, an instrument was designed containing paragraphs on specific issues to which people could react, as well as columns for indication of agreement, priority, and programming approach. Areas covered were general trends and sharp issues facing all society, church concerns needing strengthening or eliminating, programming approach for the denomination, and priorities. Space was provided for written comments and additional suggestions. Over 22,000 of these instruments were ordered and used. Though they were designed for individuals, about 60 percent were used as a basis for group discussion and response. Reporting groups varied in size from 6 to over 300.

As another approach, an invitation was issued to attend hearings in many parts of the country. Some hearings were conducted by national church staff, some by local leaders. Several bishops set up "listening posts." In west Kansas, hearings were held in twenty-eight carefully selected local churches under the leadership of program director Bruce Blake and a conference planning committee. Such hearings were kept as unstructured as possible. In all, summaries of over 100 hearings are included in the data. Hearing groups varied in size from 20 to 150 participants.

About These Data

Data from the tear sheets were prepared for processing by the Section of Research. Computer print-outs were received

15

by sex, age, marital status, laity-clergy, seven sizes of church, ten sizes of community, national staff/local church, five regions of the country, and eighty-two of United Methodism's local annual conferences.[3] "Weighted values" of responses were prepared in order that priorities and agreement could be evaluated from the proper perspective of total response, rather than simply by item count.

Material from the field instruments was collated and compared with that from the tear sheets. All written comments were read by the author—a task requiring several months and resulting in the conclusion that high priority should be given to a crash course in handwriting for United Methodists. The clearly legible comments were like a breath of fresh air in a Los Angeles smog!

The written comments are some of the most important data received. Without them we could not accurately interpret the response. For that reason the comments most indicative of the majority are used throughout this book. For the most part, comments that resulted from group discussion and consensus are used. A few individual comments of special interest are included.

The importance of the comments for interpretation can be seen, for example, in connection with a section on evangelism. From the low priority given the matter by respondents, one could easily have jumped to the conclusion that evangelism had been rejected. The written comments, however, indicated a resistance to the term "evangelism," rather than to the subject area itself.

The material from the tear sheets and the field instruments is augmented by results of the hearings. Data summaries from annual conferences that have done samplings of their own are also important sources. Two such groups distributed an

---

[3] In United Methodism, an annual conference is the basic body of the denomination. Membership is made up of the ministers and the lay delegates from a group of local churches, usually numbering several hundred. The conference meets each year to conduct basic denominational business.

instrument, prepared with professional assistance, to as many members of local parishes as possible. Those conferences are developing local church profiles for their own planning process. Such data are a valuable cross-reference.

The data were carefully summarized and analyzed. A group of national United Methodist leaders pored over the responses for a week, and a group of local church members and clergy discussed the data for another week. Conclusions on emerging priorities were then tested with United Methodist churchmen and churchwomen across the nation. In the retesting, there is 97 percent agreement that the analysis states loudly and clearly the present denominational attitudes.

On Gathering and Using Attitudes

There are great differences of opinion on how to gather attitudinal data. Attitudinal researchers do not agree on methods or on the kind of research instruments that are most valid. This fact is reflected in the comment of one professional researcher who said, upon examining the field instrument used in this sample, "This is the worst such instrument that I ever saw—except for all other such instruments that I ever saw." Following the last mayoral election in New York City, about which many major polls had made predictions, we were told that the "poll" which most nearly predicted the percentage of Mayor Lindsay's victory was not one by the well-known pollsters but a simple summary of the feelings and projections of the mayor's own ward bosses. The best of attitudinal research, at the moment, leaves room for improvement and calls for better methods.

There are two obvious dangers in the use of such data as are gathered in this collation of attitudes. One is that they will be given too much importance. We should not be trying to develop a consensus church. That would only result in a watered-down ineffectiveness. The main agenda for the church is set by the gospel of Jesus Christ and not by the highest or lowest consensus of the membership.

17

A second danger, however, is that such data not be given the weight they *should* have. These data do help define the area in which the gospel is to be applied. The Holy Spirit leads and challenges all in the church—not just top leadership—to mission. Responsibility to seek relevant involvement for a denomination rests upon all, not just a few. The insights of all, therefore, are important. The people need the stimulation of leadership. But also, leadership needs the stimulation of the people. Together, churchmen and churchwomen must weigh data on trends, issues, and church needs in the light of the purpose of the Christian church.

This is not a scientific research project. No direct distribution of the sampling instruments was made by either the Research or the Planning sections and no national probability sample was developed.[4] The data result simply from an invitation to participate, through instruments sent only upon request.

The response has been astonishing. At first, we hoped to receive, at most, substantive expressions from twenty to twenty-five of United Methodism's eighty-three annual conferences. At the date of writing, responses have come in from eighty-two, and the material from seventy-five of them is considered substantive. One bishop wrote, "This is the widest response that I have ever observed in The United Methodist Church or in the former Methodist Church. I am astounded—and pleased!"

Interestingly, the participation is quite in line with the denomination's national profile. Response from each geographical region is roughly proportional to the percentage of membership in that region. But I shall not bore you with mere statistical listings.

There was high participation in some annual conferences in each geographical region. New Mexico, Kansas West, Rocky Mountain, Mississippi, Northern Illinois, Western Pennsylva-

---

[4] Both a sampling and polling procedure are being developed by the denomination's Section of Research and will be in operation in the near future.

nia, New York, Northern New York, Virginia, North Georgia, Tennessee, and Michigan headed the list.

The field instrument was used voluntarily by unexpected groups. A large urban medical association discussed the concerns and submitted a group report, the comments in which are incisive and challenging. A local chapter of a national labor union also submitted a group summary, as did underground church groups, state pastors' conferences, student groups, ecumenical coalitions. So the interest goes on and on.

I consider these data to be *indicative*, not *demonstrative*. The material clearly indicates what those who chose to participate think and feel. No claim is made that the attitudes expressed in the material *prove* that all in The United Methodist Church would agree. In that sense these data may not be completely "right." But data do not have to be completely "right" to be enormously useful.

Alvin Toffler was getting at this when he said: "The maps of the world drawn by the medieval cartographers were so hopelessly inaccurate . . . that they elicit condescending smiles today when almost the entire surface of the earth has been charted. Yet the great explorers could never have discovered the New World without them. Nor could the better, more accurate maps of today have been drawn until men, working with the limited evidence available to them, set down on paper their bold conceptions of worlds they had never seen." [5]

That the approach used is *valid*, however, is demonstrated by the response. What we set out to do was done. We sought wide response. We got it. The mass of that response demands that the data be taken seriously.

But there is, I believe, another and more important reason why these data must be given great weight. That is the *internal consistency* of what is being said from all sources. In data from the tear sheet, from the field instrument, from hearings, and from summarizations of instruments other than our own, the same points emerge. All the data focus on the same issues, a clear indication of their reliability.

[5] Toffler, *Future Shock* (New York: Random House, 1970), p. 7.

And So—

Let's look at the response and what it is saying. That is what will be of interest to you. In doing so, we shall look at some general observations drawn from months of studying and discussing the response. After that, we shall move from the general to the specific—from general trends (chapters 3 and 4), to sharp issues (chapters 5 and 6), to needs in the denomination (chapters 7 and 8). Next will be a chapter on special concerns—some "dead horses" and a few "colts aborning." The final chapter will deal with the focus that seems to be indicated by the overall response.

As we look at what these data are saying, I would paraphrase from the Attitudinal Profile Report submitted by the Pacific Northwest Annual Conference: "The views and opinions in this summary are those of the persons and groups who chose to participate. They are not necessarily those of the author, nor will they necessarily be reflected in later samples. That is what it means to be human. We have the capacity to receive new information, consider it, and change!"

2
SOME HIT TUNES

In constructing a new home there is need to check that the building is square. The checking is not intended to tear down the building. It has the purpose of insuring that the building follows the lines set down by the architect.
—Richard Sommerfeld, *The Church of the 21st Century*

When I first began work on the data, I fully expected to find radical regional differences on denominational priorities for the 70s. But that preconception soon went out the window. Sectionalism? Not so! All regions—"jurisdictions" in United Methodist terminology—agree on priorities. Even more surprisingly, respondents agree on the order of priorities.

The general trends on which the regions focus most attention are continuing cries from persons to be fully human, cultural gaps in society, increasing secularity, continuing high rates of change, and the trend by groups to organize intentionally to bring change.

The issues to which all regions give priority are minority group demands and the church's response to them, world peace and the morality of war, living in a time of possible total extinction of the human race, the cheapness with which human life is held today, and family life/sex patterns and life styles.

More specific "churchly" priorities are the need for more laity involvement at all levels of decision-making, seeking commitment to God and a resulting commitment to service, dealing with the crisis in the professional ministry, clarifying communication channels in the church, and the need for more opportunities to designate funds as a part of responsible involvement. Work with youth, curriculum materials for Christian education, and ecumenical relations are lifted up spontaneously by respondents.

The thread of agreement runs through a majority of all responses. All annual conferences agree that the items mentioned above are of the greatest concern to their people, though a few would reorder them slightly. In two annual conferences sharp differences of opinion are expressed between the conference leaders and the rest of the conference. This indicates a rather serious communication gap in those places.

Groups such as the New Mexico Annual Conference, where the program director, Dr. Milton Chester, stimulated wide involvement; Baldwin Community United Methodist Church in Pittsburgh, where Dr. John Warman is minister; a group of students at Garrett Theological Seminary in Evanston, Illinois; and an undergraduate student group in Oklahoma—all agreed on the major areas of concern. A majority of national board staff agree, which sheds doubt on the widespread assumption of major differences of opinion between denominational leaders and persons in the local parish.

Sharp differences appear in regard to one matter only—how to go about dealing with the priorities. Local parishes demand more autonomy and more participation in decision-making, while leadership proclaims that local churches need strong direction. "There needs to be strong advocacy of Christian positions and needed programs," say the staff. "There will be less and less implementation of ideas and programs," say the membership and clergy, "unless we participate in making the decisions!" Yet the two positions may not be as polarized as they appear. A working relationship should be achieved with a little effort on both sides, since both sides agree on priorities. Participation in planning should help prepare the way for the acceptance of strong leadership but a less bureaucratic style.

"Get Our Opinions into the Pot"

The large majority of respondents find participation in the process of thinking about priorities extremely helpful.

Many say that such involvement helps to reduce resistance levels between the members of the local parish and denominational church leadership. This comment from the summary of a large urban church in Mississippi is typical of a large number of such responses:

"Our discussion group on trends, issues, and needs of the church has been a redeeming experience for our church. Originally, the instrument was given to me as the president of the Women's Society. My pastor asked me to look at it and to complete it, if I wanted to. I spent an evening studying it and thinking it over. At the end of the evening I sensed my own inadequacies to deal with much of the material.

"The next morning I telephoned my pastor to discuss several of the subjects with him. Resulting from that conversation, the decision was made to invite a group of our members to come to the church to discuss the material and to mark the paper as a group. Twenty-eight persons came together and spent an evening in the discussion.

"I admit that I was aghast upon arrival at the church to discover that the pastor had invited several of our more 'cantankerous' members to the group. At every meeting of our Administrative Board and Council on Ministries one or the other of them had loudly proclaimed antagonism, disagreement, etc., with church leadership—especially with our national boards. Each time a position has been taken by one of those boards, one of them has taken a major amount of time in our meetings to voice opposition. I feared that these persons would make our discussion unfruitful. The opposite happened!

"Each subject was fully discussed. A consensus vote was asked on how the field instrument should be marked. These persons participated fully in the discussion and were outvoted on some responses. To my amazement they did not object. When the evening discussion was ended, one of them stood and said, 'This is more like it. If they mean business, maybe our opinions can get into the pot. It's about time the national church was paying some attention to how its members feel. I hope it continues.' All I had thought so cantankerous seemed to agree. All seemed happy with the discussion, even though they were overridden on some opinions. All seemed to leave the meeting in an excellent frame of mind—the best in months.

"Thank you for letting us share in these matters with you. This has been 'cool'—to use the jargon of my teenagers."

Numerous participants express their feelings that the use of the field instrument is a stimulating and educational experience. "At least it got us to thinking about vital matters," one group says. And a medical doctor wrote on the bottom of his reply, "Two hours of stimulating fun. Thanks!" A heavy majority request continuing opportunity to express themselves.

Connectionalism OK

The field instrument gives opportunity for participants to express themselves about United Methodism's traditional connectional arrangements. Some aspects of this are that church property is not owned by a local congregation but is held in trust for the total church; ministers are not chosen by congregations but are appointed by the bishop in consultation with district superintendents and local church committees; and local churches, annual conferences, and national agencies are tied closely together in programming and mission.

An overwhelming majority of respondents indicate that they feel very comfortable with such connectionalism. They do, however, urge strongly that connectionalism be allowed to work as it was designed—with communication up as well as down.

The field instrument asks respondents to choose among the following general methods of programming: national agencies should do the programming; annual conferences should do the programming; national agencies and annual conferences together should do the programming; local churches should be left to do programming by themselves; only resources for programming should be produced; or programming should be done on a broad-based approach with government, ecumenical agencies, civic groups, and the church working together. Respondents are invited to check as many columns as they find appropriate for each concern. Their replies strongly reject the local church being turned loose to go it on its own. Very heavily favored is the local church, annual conference, and national agencies working together with more participation at all levels. Broad-based approaches are favored also, especially ecumenical coalitions to get a job done.

This response has forced me to reappraise another misconception. I had assumed that there would be more demands for congregationalism and more expressed disillusionment with the connectional system. Not so, said participants! Clean up connectionalism and allow it to operate as it was designed, with better two-way participation. "We need our national leadership," said an annual conference in the North Central Jurisdiction, "but the national leadership needs us, too! We have gotten the idea recently, however, that at least one general secretary believes that he can operate his program without us."

United Methodists voice a substantial amount of concern about the low level of confidence in the local church expressed by national staff. A comment from an annual conference in the South Central Jurisdiction is indicative of many: "We are concerned with the utter 'disdain' about the local church expressed by many of our seminaries and by our national staff. Their distaste for the local church is communicated across the church in so many overt and in so many subtle ways. The result in our conference has been noted in two reactions:

"1. Some of our members have been angered, or at least irritated, by the attitude. Therefore, they have turned off their receiving sets when seminary leaders or national leaders try to get a message through. Resulting alienation has bred a lack of confidence and therefore no communication—either way. Many of our members, so alienated, have simply written off seminary and national board leadership.

25

"2. Some of our members have been driven by this felt disdain to a feeling of hopelessness with the local church. National leaders and seminary professors have convinced knowledgeable, sensitive persons that the local church is not capable in any way of dealing with needed Christian mission today. Therefore, many of our members have withdrawn from activity in the local situation, waiting for a miracle from 'up there' in the seminary or a national board. How is this to happen? Are national boards naïve enough to believe that they can be the church by themselves? How will implementation occur if this disdain continues to drive members into hopelessness—which it is doing? How will resources for operation be found except from local churches? Do our national agencies have huge operating reserves somewhere? The local church is beginning to loudly question providing resources any longer to those who express disdain for their very existence!"

In other words, although connectionalism is strongly reaffirmed, its proper workings need "a tune-up and an oil change," which my old jalopy needs at regular intervals.

Hopelessness, Not Apathy?

The last-quoted comment brings out another dimension that generally permeates the data. Much of what the denomination has called *apathy* should more accurately be called a feeling of *hopelessness*.

The data indicate awareness, interest, and concern on the part of most respondents—hardly apathy. Yet they also indicate hopelessness about how to go about dealing with issues of which people are aware. Many local church groups appear to feel hopeless about the possibilities of acting creatively—or at all—in their own situation.

A large number of comments indicate hopelessness about influencing local church leadership to do what needs to be done. Most of these indicate that a small group of local church leaders are more interested in dictating than in listening to the desires of the membership. Some feel as do members of one local church study group, who write, "Suggestions to our leaders for trying new approaches to worship and for trying new ways and times for study are interpreted by them as an immediate threat to destroy what we have. There is no understanding that we might do both—and more." A great number feel that the pastor is too easily influenced by a few members with money who threaten to withdraw their support if any changes are made. Most feel that the gospel is sacred but that our understanding, proclamation, study, and application of it leave much to be desired. Respondents do not express hope that much can be done about it.

Just as hopeless are comments about the annual conferences and national agencies of the church. A comment from an annual conference summary in the North Central Jurisdiction seems to pull the feeling together.

"There is prevalent with individuals in our annual conference a feeling of *hopelessness*. Our conclusion after holding hearings throughout our conference, in many different settings, is as follows:

"1. Many laymen and ministers feel hopeless in the present situation because they also feel powerless. This powerlessness seems to result from their opinion that they are not listened to as decisions are made on pronouncements, programs, and commitment of funds. They feel completely ignored and unable to do anything about it.

"2. A large number of our laymen suggested using the principles of community organization to organize themselves as a group to demand that their opinions be given attention. The budding of several group caucuses within the annual conference is already noted.

"3. A significant number of our laymen seem to be immobilized by guilt feelings because of what church leadership has said to them recently about 'white racism,' 'white, middle-class Anglo-Saxonism,' 'paternalism,' and 'preoccupation with institutional maintenance.' Their expression leads us to feel that they have concluded that church leadership at all

27

levels does not feel that the average member is qualified to do anything today.

"4. The immobilization of some, however, seems to be better explained by a lack of confidence that church leadership will actually listen to their opinions. They are suspicious that expressed desires for their participation are but excuses to 'shove something else down their throats.' Before they will have any confidence in participation, we shall need to convince them that their participation will be authentic."

Who Cares?

The computer print-outs of response by size of church, in conjunction with comments from the same participants, indicate that:

1. Churches of less than fifty members seem concerned only with keeping "the door open and shingles on the roof." Most see no chance for growth in membership at their location. Therefore, pastoral leadership and program is not as important as is "no one should close us up!" Great emotion is expressed at this point, especially if the church administers a cemetery. Such churches as these express little interest in issues or needs beyond "the ends of their own noses."

2. In the responses from churches of fifty to five hundred members, high interest in trends, issues, and needs is expressed. Such churches seem sensitive to what is happening in the world and in society around them and to the needs in their own congregations.

3. Churches of five hundred to one thousand members express much less sensitivity to trends and issues than they do to their own institutional needs. They, too, are extremely concerned with maintenance of buildings and with paying for such buildings. Less concern for community issues and mission to others is expressed. Many such churches seem to feel that they should be "relieved of denominational apportionments, allowed to pay our debt, helped to get more staff, and left

28

alone to get more members," as one local church Council on Ministries said it.

4. From churches larger than one thousand members more expressions of sensitivity to trends and issues are again received. Most express a need for their church to be concerned for the persons about them as well as their institutional needs.

These responses indicate that those who believe that apathy and lack of concern center in the small church are in error. More apathy is found in medium-sized churches that may have overextended themselves with buildings.

The Seminary-Parish Gap

The instruments did not invite specific comment about seminaries and theological education. Yet, significantly, written comments on seminaries and theological education number among the highest received on any subject.

Before I had finished reading all the written comments from across the country, I reflected in an interview for *Together* magazine that a large number of such comments indicate a serious gap between theological seminaries and the church at large.[1] Additional responses since that time show a similar feeling. When attitudes expressed were retested with leadership in many of the annual conferences, there was widespread agreement that those leaders were frequently hearing the same opinion.

Comments most representative of a majority of the written expressions include the following from an annual conference summary in the Southeastern Jurisdiction:

"There is an obvious gap between the seminary desk theology and the practical working theology of the parish. We see lessening practical relationship between seminary training and the work in our local churches. Certainly, the seminarian shows little understanding, and littler patience, with persons where they are! He comes to us prepared for a ministry that is not

[1] See "Changes United Methodists Want in Their Church," *Together*, December, 1970, p. 10.

29

relevant for the situation in which he finds himself. The young minister is soon frustrated. The people in the parish are even more frustrated. Little happens except alienation. The laymen are often more deeply entrenched in their old ways, sinful though they be. Is that leadership? We don't think so! Seminaries should prepare ministers for situations that exist—not what some professor in his ivory tower idealistically and paternalistically wishes to exist. Our churches are demanding seminary men less and less."

Even more caustic was a comment from the northeastern part of the country, where an annual conference group summary said: "Our seminaries are little monastic orders where more and more the seminary monks are interested in talking to themselves only. They are afraid to put their thought in common language. Their associates would deem that a sellout. Seminaries do not prepare ministers for the local church but rather for anything else. Seminaries are no longer serving The United Methodist Church."

The attitudes expressed in these comments are repeated in different ways by many participants, including those who spoke out at hearings throughout the United States. One annual conference in the south central United States held hearings in twenty-eight carefully selected local churches. In addition to stating their feelings about the isolation and insulation of the seminary from the local church, participants reacted strongly to the "faddism in theology" of our times. They see seminary professors as afraid to allow their writing and their position to stay the same tomorrow as it is today. "Theological seminaries have a low level of goodwill among laymen," their hearing summary says.

Numerous suggestions for changes in seminary education were received. Most numerous is that professors serve a local church either continuously or during a sabbatical every few years. Many think that this should be as important as continuing academic education. Also suggested is that seminarians be required to serve a local church as "a part of seminary education." A majority want the denomination to work toward less isolation of the seminary from the local church.

New Concepts for the Rural Church

High concern is voiced in many of United Methodism's annual conferences about rural parishes. Many feel that the denomination has become enamored of urban and inner-city ministries to the neglect of the rural. From one annual conference a group asks, "Have we forgotten that United Methodism is still mostly rural? Why are we not giving rural churches better leadership?"

In the summary of a wide sampling in an annual conference in the Northeastern Jurisdiction we find the thinking of most respondents pulled together:

"We believe that The United Methodist Church must re-evaluate the importance of the rural church for the future. We suggest the following for consideration:

"1. Too often we bemoan the situation in the rural church today, saying that it is not worthy of our best leadership. We are overly critical of members who are emotionally tied to those churches and who make great sacrifices to keep those churches operating. A better approach would be to provide the best leadership, highly trained, to *lead* the rural church to a solution of its own problems. Well-trained rural coordinators would cost far less in the long run than continuing mission support of small rural churches. Many such churches can be led together: they cannot be driven! In addition, having such leadership would excite those in the rural church who now feel completely unwanted, ignored, and therefore defensive.

"2. Develop new models for rural parishes. Get some working! New models will help get done what needs to be done. No amount of pamphlets, conferences, or browbeating will do it. 'Build a better mousetrap,' it has been said, 'and people will beat a path to your door.'

"3. Be alert to the fact, as Lyle Schaller points out in his book *The Impact of the Future*, that rapidly increasing num-

31

bers of urban residents are moving out of the city into rural areas and establishing residence. Projected 'strip cities' will engulf many rural churches in the near future. Provide leadership in such areas that will be able to minister to these new residents and the *old as well*. To this point we have missed the boat on this one."

Valid concerns are being voiced in such comments. Some are trying to build models. The Rev. Lloyd Wright, on the program staff in southern Indiana, has been leading rural churches into new concepts. Others will need to give the full-time attention to these churches that he is giving, respondents indicate.

3
TRENDS: THE TOP OF THE HEAP

> We are now living through the second great divide in human history, comparable in magnitude only with that first break in historic continuity—the shift from barbarism to civilization. . . .
>
> The mood, the pace, the very "feel" of existence, as well as one's underlying notions of time, beauty, space and social relations will be shaken.
>
> —Alvin Toffler, "The Future as a Way of Life," *Horizon*, Summer, 1964

The two written instruments and the series of hearings brought forth a flood of opinion from United Methodists all over the fifty states. Participants were invited to react to brief written statements in three areas: general trends, sharp issues, and church needs. This chapter and the next will take a look at United Methodist reaction to statements about general trends. They will quote a number of comments, from groups and some individuals, all of which are typical of the written and spoken feelings of many other participants.

Trends are defined on the field instrument as "identifiable, general, prevailing tendencies in our culture most likely to continue into the years 1972-1976." The trends discussed in these two chapters are the ones presented to participants for reaction. Though space was provided for listing additional trends, no others were mentioned often enough to supplant any on the original list. The order of priority given here is the order expressed in the responses.

1. Cries for humanization will continue.
2. Gaps in our culture will continue to need attention.

3. Secularity will continue to grow.
4. The rate of change will continue to accelerate.
5. Groups will intentionally organize to effect change.
6. New institutional forms will be sought.
7. Knowledge will increase rapidly.
8. Mixing of all cultures will take place.
9. Communications networks will be a growing influence.

1. Humanization: "I'm Not a Number, I'm a Me"

The paragraph about humanization to which participants responded spoke of cries from humans for equality in court, at work, in housing, in education, and in distribution of wealth. Also included were cries for the freedom to congregate, cries for freedom from dehumanizing impersonal systems, cries to be treated with respect as human beings, and cries for all humans to use integrity in dealing with others.

The replies expressed overwhelming agreement that humanization has the highest priority among the trends for church programming. With the figure 1 being the highest weighted value for the 9 trends, the respondents give humanization a weight of 1.32. Comparison print-outs indicate that all agree on this priority. The feeling also comes through that influencing this trend will take the best efforts of the denomination at all levels *plus* ecumenical efforts and work with government agencies.

A majority of expressions indicate a tremendous frustration with the feeling that man is becoming more and more just "part of the crowd," "another grain of sand on the beach," "a number in the classroom," "a cog in a something's (not even a someone's) wheel." Reflects one university student, "When my number is called in class or I'm asked for my student identification number when cashing a check, I feel like screaming anymore, 'I'm not a number, I'm me!'" And as she screams, she will be in chorus with most. Respondents also agree, "We cannot buy our way out of the crowd." "Only as persons are treated as persons with genuine concern and with

34

equity will a human order emerge from the present impersonal chaos."

Cries like these must be heard. In a sermon entitled "The Sounds of Silence," the Rev. Allan Wilson of Indiana spoke incisively of "hearing without hearing." After Paul Simon's song with the same title, sung by a group of youth, the sermon continued, "How long? Paul Simon says that people cannot keep silent forever. 'Silence like a cancer grows.' It will find ears to hear or hearts to feel, or it will smolder and fume and finally explode.

"Are these legitimate examples of too much silence or not? —you be the judge: riots in our cities, rebellion on our campuses, Catholic-Protestant trouble in Ireland, the sex revolution, the youth rebellion, socialism, juvenile delinquency. . . . How long will it take us to see that while it is surely painful to listen openly to, and speak honestly to, and understand deeply the cries of those in our homes, our communities, and our world, it is far more constructive a way than waiting for life to tumble in all around us!"

The continuing cry for humanization is seen by most as a call to recognize the great worth of the individual as a person. Dr. Grover Hartman, executive secretary of the Indiana Council of Churches, catches what most are saying: "We do not see every person as being of infinite worth and as having potential for highly significant growth and contribution to our community. So long as we have a low view of persons we will not be deeply enough concerned with children—black or white —to attack the problem of limited educational opportunities in inner-city areas, not concerned enough to move effectively against discrimination in employment or vocational training which handicaps some of our youth and adults economically, not concerned enough with recipients of public assistance to seek means to meet their needs while maintaining their dignity and self-respect, not concerned enough with youth falling into delinquency and adults convicted of crime to work creatively

35

for crime prevention and for genuine rehabilitation." [1] "Treat each person as of infinite worth" is the cry-havoc running through the responses.

Appearing repeatedly in the comments is the feeling that the denomination must deal with humanization as a prerequisite to all else. Many voice a belief that a lack of real caring for persons and a denial of their infinite worth are largely responsible for the ineffectiveness of the church's evangelism. As one reply says: "If The United Methodist Church could give four years to depth study and broad application of what it means to regard fellowmen as truly human, we would go a long way toward real commitment to evangelism. For we would see man as a valuable soul needing to be related to God as a necessity for fulfillment of his or her personhood. Solution of our acute social problems would then begin to appear, because we would begin to regard each person as a 'somebody'!"

Many agree that the denomination, in its institutional and bureaucratic operation, is itself one of the worst dehumanizers of persons. We have already seen this dimension clearly in the comments about hopelessness. From the summary of a large group of local church hearings in the south central region comes this comment, indicative of many others:

"The church itself is one of the greatest offenders in the dehumanization of people. She has often been guilty of developing and maintaining congregational 'castes' based on race or economic status. She has been guilty of using persons for her own purposes. She has been and is guilty of a dehumanizing paternalism which attempts to determine mission for or to others without their own involvement in the decisions about their own destiny. Church leadership has a lot to learn about listening *to* persons and about working *with* persons. Too often leadership, by attitude at least, communicates that all others should 'be good and do things the way we tell you to!' Yes,

---

[1] Excerpt from a speech prepared by Dr. Hartman for Radio Station WXLW, Indianapolis, Indiana.

The United Methodist Church should be for humanization with great priority—*but in her own house first.*"

When I first read this comment publicly as part of an oral summary, a "liberated woman" in attendance objected strenuously to referring to the church in such a negative context and at the same time as "she." "If the denomination had had more feminine characteristics over the years," she said, "we would have been treating persons as persons."

An unsolicited comment on humanization comes from Isaiah.

> Is not this what I require of you as a fast:
>   to loose the fetters of injustice,
>   to untie the knots of the yoke,
>   to snap every yoke
>   and set free those who have been crushed?
> Is it not sharing your food with the hungry,
> taking the homeless poor into your house,
>   clothing the naked when you meet them
>   and never evading a duty to your kinsfolk?
> Then shall your light break forth like the dawn
> and soon you will grow healthy like a wound newly healed;
>   your own righteousness shall be your vanguard
>   and the glory of the Lord your rearguard.
>   (Isaiah 58:6-8 NEB)

2. Culture Gaps: Living with Our Differences

"It seems to us," say a group of students in the far west, "that the so-called gaps in our society could all be summarized under 'cultural gaps.' Each gap may have dimensions of its own, but each may be characterized as a failure of communication of one cultural pattern with another. Conditioned by that one culture pattern, persons find it difficult to understand what another culture is saying. Defensive about the rightness of their own ways, persons find that 'cultural shock'[2] keeps

[2] Alvin Toffler in *Future Shock*, p. 12, defines cultural shock as the effect that immersion in a strange culture has on the unprepared visitor. The results are bewilderment, frustration, and a breakdown in communication.

them from readily accepting another's cultural position. Let the church work on leading her people in an understanding of and an appreciation of other cultural patterns." Such a comment is typical of what most respondents are saying.

Participants were invited to reflect on the gaps existing in the culture today, on polarization between those of opposing viewpoints, and on extremism. The following gaps were given a great deal of attention in the written comments:

1. A gap between the generations. Indications are that this is seen as a gap between youth and parents rather than a simple age gap. Youth and older persons, fifty-five and older, seemed to agree on most questions. The age group of forty-five through fifty-four, however, often disagrees with both. This seems to bear out the feeling of the students that the gap is more of cultural patterns than of age.

2. A gap between those of differing theological and ideological viewpoints. Some comments in this category indicate extreme intolerance for any theological or ideological viewpoint except that held by the one responding.

3. A gap between the affluent and the poor. Many express the feeling that a more equitable distribution of wealth must be found. This expression is voiced most often by youth and by older people.

4. A credibility gap between denominational leadership and the average church member. Written comments indicate that each feels that the other holds them in disdain. A summary from a large lay group expresses their feelings: "The most serious gap is the credibility gap between leadership and average church members. Members have been manipulated so much and for so long that there is no confidence that any proposal now made by leadership will not result in more of the same. Many members feel that church leadership believes that *only* leadership is capable of making decisions about what the church should be doing. Thus, decisions about programming are made that get increasingly less implementation. But, there is one decision that the average member is coming to realize that he is perfectly capable of making. That is the

38

decision as to where he shall commit his time, energy, and money. More and more his commitment is going where the average member feels that he is more appreciated, and where he feels more involved in meaningful ways."

Although many different views are expressed about the gaps of our culture, there is striking agreement at one point: "No attempt should be made to 'water everyone down' to a common viewpoint." The existence of many viewpoints, and the cross-fertilization among them, is seen by most participants as highly desirable. One annual conference Board of Missions commented as follows: "The United Methodist Church should be big enough to make room for persons and groups of differing theological and ideological viewpoints. Let the church stop treating those who differ in approach with our bureaucrats as though they were second-class citizens. Let our church bureaucrats . . . stop reacting to those who differ with . . . [their] views as though the poor, stupid things don't have sense enough to come in out of the rain! There is value in the cross-fertilization of differing views. Let The United Methodist Church make such differences an authentic witness of sincere people."

3. Growing Secularity in the Promised Land

Respondents say loud and clear that secular life is more and more setting the tone of all life, that value systems are being changed by secular considerations, and that it is increasingly true that only the message which is put into the secular language of everyday experience can be clearly communicated.

It is apparent from the data that persons above the age of 55 see secularity and its influence as being more urgent than do others. Males as a group drop consideration of secularity much farther down, to seventh in their priority list. Apparently they feel more comfortable in a secular world than do older people as a group.

Secularization has been defined as man turning his atten-

39

tion away from worlds beyond and toward this world and this time. It is said to deliver man from religious and other-worldly control over his reason and his language. For some, secularization merely compartmentalizes religion, bypasses it as innocuous, and goes on to more "practical" things. For others, secularization is a challenge to seek ways of communicating Christian truth in the jargon of the secular. In particular, elements of secular experience that cannot be adequately explained by secular thought are sought by some participants, who wish to communicate the gospel better. These elements, such as hope, anxiety, brokenness, and shaping the future, give unique opportunity for Christian faith and experience to speak.

Respondents seem to be deeply committed to the urgency of a more relevant relationship between the Christian church and the secular society. Most feel that The United Methodist Church is too isolated within its buildings. Members of the denomination must, many say, be more involved as practicing Christians in the secular world if the Christian gospel is to be communicated. "Man cannot," says one group, "wash his brother's feet from an easy chair or from a pulpit."

Most respondents, however, believe Christians must "remember that the message is God's." An annual conference group from South Central puts it this way: "Secularity must be dealt with. It must not be allowed to set the tone of the Christian life. The secular will, however, alert us to new approaches and will give us new language with which to communicate Christian truth. Nevertheless, the message is God's no matter what the vocabulary! The church must always remember that she is called in every secular situation to proclaim, 'At this time and in this place there is a word from on high!' "

Many say that they feel The United Methodist Church has too often acted as though the message as well as the vocabulary is secular. "If we yield to that temptation," say a large number, "the church no longer has reason to exist." Secular institutions can convey the secular message better than the church ever can, they feel. Let the church convey the message of God, but convey it in every vocabulary, every thought form, every art form available. Discard old forms when they no longer speak. Use new forms when they do. But keep the message clear!

4. The World Changes as We Walk in It

Voiced widely is the feeling that nothing is permanent anymore except change. Change has always been with us; the rapidity of it has not. This caused physicist Robert Oppenheimer to say, "One thing that is new is the prevalence of newness, the changing scale and scope of change itself, so that the world alters as we walk in it."

In an editorial, "Life Inside a Centrifuge," Norman Cousins once observed: "Into a few decades have been compressed more change, more thrusts, more tossing about of men's souls and gizzards than have been spaced out over most of the human chronicle until now. The entire metabolism of history has gone berserk." Many United Methodists would agree.

The escalating dimensions of change are widely heralded in the literature of the day. One half of all the energy that man has consumed in the past two thousand years has been used in the last one hundred, we are told. One fourth of all the people who ever lived are alive today. Ninety percent of all the scientists who ever lived are now at work. Technical information now doubles at the rate of every ten years.

The present becomes the past as we touch it. No longer can any institution operate on the theory that society is relatively static. Straight-line projections of present trends have little validity. The trends will have changed before the projection has been widely communicated.

Often, therefore, we find ourselves unready to meet the future when it arrives. Confusion, frustration, disorientation, and shock result. We find ourselves discussing "future shock," "cultural shock," and all the rest.

Many respondents express the opinion that the church is set up more to resist rapid change than to work with it, more to protect the old (the change of another generation) than to

41

move out with vital Christian truth into the new (the change of this and coming generations). These respondents say that only recently has the denomination begun to take seriously the planning and research functions and that it is yet too early to know whether such functions will meet with response. At least two factors must be overcome, many reflect, before we can deal with change.

First, there is the fear of the new, an integral part of human response. "Taking a new step, uttering a new word, is what people fear most," said Dostoevsky. And Eric Hoffer observes: "We can never be really prepared for that which is wholly new. We have to adjust ourselves, and every radical adjustment is a crisis of self-esteem. . . . It needs inordinate self-confidence to face drastic change without inner trembling." As individuals, most of us find old ways more comfortable—like old shoes. We have to develop self-confidence to face rapid change. And we do not know how much can be done. Toynbee raises the question, "Is there not a limit to the amount of change in the environment that a human being can digest within a lifetime?" We do not know the answer, but we must seek it.

Second, many people now see the church as an institution for preserving what were at one time great changes in the ethical and moral values of men. For such persons revelation, and the institution called to protect it, are seen as static. To them God has spoken; he is not now speaking. That God still reveals himself, that the denomination must move out on the attack as did founder Wesley, rather than fall back on defensive entrenchments, must be recognized. So say many thoughtful participants.

"To protect themselves against further change, institutions harden their resistance by formalizing rituals, customs and traditions. In a rapidly changing technology, the social organism thus preserved becomes unable to cope with its new environment and either must give way to the innovators, or fail to survive." [3]

[3] Don Fabun, *The Dynamics of Change* (Englewood Cliffs, N. J.: Prentice-Hall, 1968), p. I-9.

One group of respondents in the southeast urge in their summary that the denomination start immediately to differentiate in its tradition between what is truth and what is just archaic practice. We might, they say, find food for thought in the following story from Russia at the time of the czars.

In the beautiful park of St. Petersburg's Winter Palace there was a beautiful lawn, on that lawn a bench, next to that bench two guards. Every three hours the guards were changed. No one knew why! But one day an ambitious young lieutenant was put in charge of the Palace Guard. Being of enquiring mind, he began to ask questions. In the end, a cobwebby little old man, The Palace Historian, was found. "Yes," the old man said, "there is a reason. During the reign of Peter the Great some 200 years ago, the bench got a coat of paint. Fearing that the ladies-in-waiting might get paint on their gowns, the czar ordered a guard to the bench. The order was never rescinded. In 1908 all guards at the palace were doubled in fear of revolution. The bench has been doubly guarded ever since."

Large numbers of respondents see the denomination "standing guard" on outmoded practices without really knowing why.

Most participants in the sampling feel that the denomination must reevaluate all that it is doing in the light of the gospel and the rapid changes of the times. "The willingness to experiment and innovate will be necessary if the church is to relate realistically to accelerating change. If the church attempts to only maintain the old ways and to do only the same old thing, a rapidly changing society will simply pass it by on the way to the twenty-first century," says an annual conference group in the west. "We must learn to make present decisions which may influence the probabilities change-wise of tomorrow. Let's not just try to react to, and keep abreast of, change," advises an individual who identifies himself as a member of a corporate planning team.

We are aiming neither to lament nor to rhapsodize about change, but to discern its character for the purpose of shaping the goals and strategies appropriate for the denomination's continuing mission. Whatever the specific nature of change, the faithful church needs to be conscious of God's continuing shaping of history, in an effort to discover both the qualities from the past that should be preserved and the cues that call for movement into the future. While change may alter the form of human need and the shape in which the truth of God's love will be affirmed, the church is called to the continuing tasks of worship, witness, and service in forms appropriate to the age. In the words of a familiar hymn, "New occasions teach new duties."

5. Group Power: "Here Come da Troops"

In giving this trend fifth priority, respondents are reacting to confrontations in the denomination by group caucuses organized for that purpose, to community organization groups bringing their power to bear upon society, and to deliberate group pressure upon government as a growing phenomenon. The feeling is high that such group activity will continue both in and outside of denominational meetings. "The church must plan how she shall receive such groups and also how she shall participate in some of them," say many respondents. Many believe that the growing proliferation of such groups may eventually neutralize their effectiveness: "Too many crying wolf will tend to be nonproductive." A great majority of all comments reject violence as an accepted method of group operation.

A large group of the denomination's Women's Society officers in the southeast ask: "Isn't the church a prime example of a group intentionally organized to bring change? The idea is not frightening when it is understood in those positive terms, is it?" Others responding in like manner state strongly the belief that the church is not the church when it fails to plan for change and to use its group power to effect planned change.

The feeling that groups will continue to organize to effect change is evident in this expression from a group summary in the Oklahoma Indian Mission: "Groups will organize. To wait for the establishment to do something on its own is to wait for doomsday. They buy you off with pacifiers which are sour pickles in one's mouth. The church talks, studies, writes papers, but it does not move. It makes good statements but continues its business as usual. It appeases but serves only itself. So, groups will organize."

A group from one annual conference in the north central area observes: "This is happening very swiftly in our annual conference! Caucuses of many types are springing up. No longer do Methodists for Church Renewal have the field all to themselves. Now we have evangelicals, youth, blacks, inner city, and other groups getting organized. There is even the threat to organize a group against organized groups. Group organization will be more and more a phenomenon at all levels —even at General Conference. Here come da troops!"

Others indicate that now that they have been taught to use group organization to effect change, they plan to use it to confront national boards in The United Methodist Church. Indicative of many such expressions is this from an urban missionary society in a large midwestern city: "The Board of Missions has taught us to use group organization and economic boycott as effective tools to get attention for group feelings and effect change. We have found that it works with local government, businesses, etc. We wonder if it would work in the church? We're going to try—even with the paternalistic Board of Missions." Similar statements were made about influencing the church school curriculum and other general agencies. Here come da troops indeed.

4
TRENDS: DIGGING ON DOWN

> And then, if we are even faintly serious about the altered society we foresee, we must allow time and means for the alteration of men to fit that society. And men are not to be altered like armaments—by scrapping what is no longer apt and "refitting" what is only in part so. If the changes envisioned are far-reaching, new men must be grown—by men willing and able to undergo the agony of making themselves over so far as they are able, even while they must foster, and subsequently tolerate, what is newer, and hence more alien, yet.
> —John R. Seeley, "Time's Future in Our Time"

Although the thousands of United Methodists who shared their attitudes give higher priority to the trends discussed in the preceding chapter, those same respondents also take the time to write comments about the four that follow. These comments should therefore be considered seriously in any planning for the future.

6. New Institutions: More Business as Usual?

Respondents in this sampling seem quite suspicious of institutional forms. Time and again they say that new forms, either in or out of the church, will result in nothing more than reshuffling, with business continuing largely as usual. Respondents are not begging for the status quo. Neither do they see virtue in tinkering with institutional machinery. "Let's clean up the institutions that we have," says one group, "and get at the issues!"

A sizable group of respondents who see the need for new and different institutions in society strongly advocate letting such institutions grow out of function. This group gives low priority to the trend, because they feel that any attempt to design new institutions by a committee, or a conference, will result in "a four-headed monster fighting with itself over which head has the right to devour the rest of society." "If we get about the business of a better life for all humans, the best institutions will emerge."

There is much feeling, however, that more flexible and more responsive institutional forms are needed and that they will evolve because they must. "And when they do evolve," says a group of annual conference youth, "we shall not mourn the passing of the old. Those institutions will have served their time. We agree with Alexis de Tocqueville when he said, 'I am tempted to believe that what we call necessary institutions are often no more than institutions to which we have grown accustomed.'"

The responses point out the inflexibility of present institutions of society as shown by the large amount of "lead time" needed to implement changes. "Congress is always legislating to cope with the needs of the last decade," says one group. "They need ten years lead time to deal with present social reality." One bishop speaks of even longer delays in The United Methodist Church. "Look at the record," he says. "The General Conference takes twelve years to study and debate before they implement major changes."

The tendency of all organizations to proliferate into a myriad of suborganizations calls forth many objections. "It happens in our conference. It happens in the national organization of Methodism. It happens in local government, national government—you name it. It happens! Interboards, what-have-you. And each one thinks they are indispensable. Usually, they are a confession of outdated organization that is no longer functional!"

Dr. Bigelow Wynkoof, an acknowledged expert on the life style of the middle-aged, spoke to this tendency of organizations to proliferate in a much discussed article, "The Pooped Generation":

47

"Organizations tend to call forth organizations. . . . Look back 30 years. If a boy wanted to play ball, he and his friends walked down to a vacant lot and started a game of One Old Cat. For this they needed no uniforms, no committees, no secretary or treasurer—at most they needed a ball, bat and three or four gloves. But look at the situation today—Little Leagues all over, coaches, managers, committees, regular practice, scheduled games, championships, mothers and fathers driving all over, meetings and so forth." [1]

Quite a number of comments reflect with dismay on the tendency of institutions to perpetuate themselves long after they have fulfilled their purpose. "An organization never votes itself out of business even after it has outlived its usefulness," says a student group. "It just goes on and on with its officers and staff preparing papers and calling meetings in an attempt to justify its little kingdom."

Interest in institutional forms expressed in the data could all be summed up by saying, "Forms should follow function. Function should be determined by quick responsiveness to need. But, don't proliferate the forms. When a form has fulfilled its need, get rid of it."

7. The Knowledge Explosion

Participants who commented on this trend were reflecting on the rapid growth of knowledge, the fact that computerization of knowledge raises questions about who shall have access to it and who shall control it, and the fact that rapidly increasing knowledge will speed the coming of change and necessitate new educational approaches.

Laity in the age group 45 through 54, and youth give the increase of knowledge much higher priority than do other respondents, possibly because they are more exposed to the trend than are others. Older laity are aware that rapidly increasing knowledge has made retraining and more education necessary just to keep them from becoming obsolete in their

[1] *Changing Times,* The Kiplinger Magazine, December, 1969, p. 8.

careers. Youth are aware that they are being exposed in their education to twice as much knowledge as was available to those who graduated in 1940 or before. Those who have need for access to computer banks of technical information report that they are already experiencing "careful screening" before that access is opened—control of knowledge. And so they feel more urgency.

Many comments indicate little comprehension of how rapidly knowledge is growing and even less awareness of the possibilities for control and determination of who shall have access to such stored knowledge.

Knowledge has doubled since 1940, we are told. Even more astounding is the projection that knowledge will again double by 1976 and again by 1980. Some of the implications of this were noted by Henri Janne, former Belgian Minister of Education: "Scientific and technical knowledge is increasing so rapidly that the 'foundation' supplied by the school soon becomes insufficient. . . . The schooling of youth will be less and less a matter of acquiring knowledge (which soon becomes outdated) and information (provided more comprehensively elsewhere) but will be devoted rather to the acquisition of methods of thought, 'adaptive' attitudes, critical reactions and disciplines which teach 'how to learn.' . . . The notion that one acquires during one's schooling a store of knowledge valid for one's whole existence has become a myth. From now on, it will be necessary to learn where and how to secure knowledge, how to select, integrate, and utilize the information acquired." [2]

By the application of available knowledge to human life and environment, man increasingly has the capacity to determine the direction in which the human race shall move. Thus, social engineers, "think centers," and organized groups with specialized knowledge effect social change. Scientists, drawing

[2] Janne, "Teaching People to Adapt to Change," *The Futurist*, June, 1970, p. 81.

upon vast knowledge, work "miracles" in biochemical, genetic, and environmental change. One unavoidable conclusion emerges: More than ever before, the capacity for total destruction or for total life seems to lie within the reach of man.

Certainly the church should have a vital role in these new emerging dimensions of living. Values must be examined by decision-makers before decisions are made. The church should point the way. It could be that the prophetic role of the church and the responsibility of witnessing to the message of the gospel will be done most effectively, not by resolutions and pronouncements that for the most part fall on deaf ears, but rather by actual involvement in society's problem-solving processes, where knowledge is the price of admission.

If so, analytical and conceptual skills for the best use of knowledge must be given priority for development. Churchmen and churchwomen will need several periods, or a continuing process, of retraining in order to maintain a high level of competency in relation to the accumulating new knowledge. Therefore, the need for continuing education will take on new dimensions of importance. A state pastors' school in the North Central Jurisdiction in speaking to this says: "The United Methodist Church must make the sabbatical year for study a practical reality. Now, there is only lip service to an impractical possibility. Any minister electing to take a sabbatical would be out in the cold upon his return. Make a year for sabbatical study a reality, with our schools designing a curriculum for that purpose. If the annual conferences would use money now being spent on ineffective continuing education to pay the salaries for a couple of ministers who could substitute for those on sabbatical (with the one on sabbatical receiving his same salary so he could support his family), effective continuing education would then take place."

Many respondents using the field instrument express more concern with using knowledge now at our fingertips than they do with worrying about additional, rapidly expanding knowledge to come. A South Central college student group in its summary states: "It would be helpful if we would show more concern for using the knowledge that we already have! We are more concerned over the prostitution of the knowledge that we have had for a long time than we are about new knowledge. Let's work on value systems to help assure proper relationships and proper use of all, whenever, wherever, however."

An annual conference Program Council in the North Central Jurisdiction expresses a widespread concern that "someone seems to be contemplating a centralized information storage bank for the denomination." They express their apprehension: "Knowledge should be stored so that all have access to the storage! Therefore, storage must be *decentralized*. We must never allow storage of knowledge to be so centralized that we are at the mercy of an 'elite few' who control the centers and what goes into them. We cannot support centralized storage of knowledge or information in the church. Already we have felt the barbs of denominational bureaucrats who felt that they knew what we should do, because they felt themselves to be more knowledgeable than we."

8. Beyond the Melting Pot

"Increasing mixing of all cultures is becoming more evident throughout the world" begins the short paragraph on the field instrument. Because of such factors as high mobility and increased communication, old cultures are losing their sharp identities. Therefore, even "greater mixing and less cultural identity may well be the picture of tomorrow."

Respondents are well aware that cultural mixing has taken place. They mention the "westernizing of Japanese culture"; "the gradual disappearance of, or, at the least, radical change of, ethnic cultures in our large cities"; and "the acceptance of 'foreign' foods, religions, and philosophies in the United States." But even while recognizing that mixing has happened and is happening, the large majority of respondents back off in fear that we may lose the values of diversity.

From every part of the country and from all groups come

51

expressions of resistance. This from Chicago is indicative: "Cultural mixing will not be allowed to happen! And, it would be undesirable if it did!"

From an annual conference in the northeast: "Cultural mixing is an issue all right. However, we see diversity and identity as values to be maintained. We should respect all cultures. We should stop attempting to impress *our* culture on other peoples and on other lands. We should not allow others to impress their culture upon us. This is not to say that we should not learn from each other: that we must do! But we do not believe that *we* should ever be a 'melting pot' for all— nor should *they*. We affirm diversity as a value to be maintained."

From a group of blacks: "Cultural mixing has been more in the picture in the past than it will be in the future. Each individual should be proud of his or her culture! Each individual should respect the culture of others. All should seek for common heritage while at the same time seeking for uniqueness in that heritage. Unique cultural identities should be maintained."

From a young adult group in South Central: "The best of all cultures should be preserved. We question whether a movement toward one world culture is the best way. Such would tend to seek the lowest and worst elements of each culture. When you water everything down to the lowest common denominator, you are likely to end up with nothing that is desirable—a colorless, monotonous, uninteresting blah! Our group feels strongly that the church should speak to the values of cultural identity."

It is obvious that respondents understood cultural mixing to imply the leveling out of all cultures into one overall culture. There was difficulty comprehending the possibility of increased cultural mixing, with learning from cultures other than our own while maintaining identity of cultures. It seems that it is for this reason that United Methodists express resistance to the idea of cultural mixing—a kind of cultural shock.

9. World Communications: Networks of Knowledge

The main elements of this trend are that because of world communication networks, it can no longer be assumed that an illiterate is unknowledgeable; levels of life expectancy are rising in all countries, because communications satellites transmit "possibilities" even to remote huts; and communications rapidly spread trends, customs, and cultures from one area of the world to another.

These concepts meet negative reaction from most of those who comment. Apparently, participants have little comprehension of the potential of world communications. Again, many comments resist the idea that communications networks might bring about the emergence of one world culture. Typical is: "Influence—yes! One culture—no!"

Yet much is happening! The evidence that, because of world communications, illiterates can no longer be considered unknowledgeable was powerfully impressed upon me in the Bolivian Andes two years ago. At the time, I lived in Montclair, New Jersey, and was employed by the United Methodist Board of Missions in New York City. My wife and I spent much of the summer at mission stations in Latin America. Gasping for oxygen one morning in Bolivia, I entered a village located high above the timberline, supposedly to discuss Christian mission in that area. But first, that was not to be. The group gathered in a stone and adobe hut had a prior concern. "They request," said my missionary host, "that we discuss the riots in Newark, for they have been told that you come from that area. What is The United Methodist Church doing in that situation?" I was embarrassed at two points. First, the denomination should have been doing more than it was. We often would rather deal with our Christian mandate for mission in Bolivia than with our mandate for mission in Newark. Second, much had happened in Newark since my departure, and they knew more about it than I did. In the corner of the hut was a six-dollar transistor radio, permanently tuned to one station, continuously blaring out the news and happenings from around the world. They had heard from Newark. Traveling, I had not. Illiterate? Mostly. Unknowledgeable? No!

It would seem that the denomination has an immediate responsibility to help members be aware of what is happening through the use of world communications networks. The people should be aware of the potential of mass media, especially that of the transistor radio found in remote huts and in coolies' breast pockets—found almost everywhere—and the rapid spread of television sets, fed who-knows-what by communications satellites. World communications are evangelizing in a sense. The church should be interested in *what* sense.

5

ISSUES: BEYOND THE GOTHIC WALLS

> Insects and birds and fish and animals live in an environment which is normal to them. Even in our city zoos we have created artificially a normal ecology for the animals. But we refuse to do it for our human brothers. For mountain goats we make some rocks to climb on; we give antelopes a park-like place with a moat around it; even the snakes enjoy air-conditioning! But we won't provide proper housing for human beings and a good community environment for our children.
> —Ted F. Silvey, AFL-CIO, "Technology and Cultural Lag," *Adult Leadership*, November, 1955

The second section of the field instrument invited United Methodists to comment on issues—"matters coming into sharp focus, the decision of which will be of vital importance to The United Methodist Church." The ten issues discussed in this chapter and the next are, in order of priority given them by participants:

1. Minority group demands and possible responses.
2. World peace and the morality of war.
3. Living with the possibility of total extinction of human life.
4. The cheapness with which human life is treated.
5. Family life and sex mores.
6. Polarization in society.
7. Man's stewardship of the environment.
8. Breakdown in communications between church and world.
9. Effects of growing automation.
10. The biomedical revolution.

Again, those who used the field instrument were invited to write in additional issues they felt were vital. The only such issues raised by any substantial number of respondents are the women's liberation movement, a point raised primarily by women, and overhaul of the nation's welfare system, one raised by a wide spectrum of individuals and groups. Most who comment upon these two issues, however, agree that they can be dealt with under demands of minority groups. Let me hasten to say, before I am scalped or treated to a karate chop, that I am well aware that "shes" are not a minority. They are a majority, as indicated in the opening chapter! They are only treated as a minority, quote, unquote. Whew! Now that the lid has been kicked off that box, we can go on.

1. The Wheel That Squeaks Get Greased

The paragraph on minority group demands in the field instrument states that demands will continue to be heard from ethnic and minority groups, that the church must be in the front lines of those who are listening and responding to those demands, and that all persons must be free to move in society with dignity, opportunity, and responsibility.

Examinations of the computer print-outs show an extremely high agreement level—97.15 percent—with the ideas expressed in that paragraph. Agreement drops only in one age group, from 45 to 54. In this group, the expressed priority for minority group demands drops drastically to fifth among their priorities, as compared to first for the denomination as a whole. One professional researcher observed that people in this age group are the ones who have most recently "made it." They are defensive about protecting "it" from any threat by any group. "They are the new establishment," he said.

That observation is reminiscent of a quotation in *Second Living Room Dialogues:* "It took me forty years to get a house in the country, two cars, and money for retirement. These things justify a life of hard work. You can't expect me to give them up." Perhaps the researcher is right.

56

More significant, however, for The United Methodist Church is the recognition that this is the group upon which the denomination relies most heavily for budgetary funds. The implications seem clear. All in The United Methodist Church are agreed that "response to minority group demands" is the highest priority issue for church programming, except the age group that members rely on to foot the bills.

The print-outs also indicate that one size-of-community group gives even lower priority to this issue. Responses from communities of ten thousand to fifty thousand largely indicate disagreement with the dimensions of the issue stated and also indicate a priority rating of eighth among the ten. In discussions of the data, several questions keep popping up: "Are these communities where confrontations are taken more personally than in larger cities?" "Are these the communities which might be centers of the so-called 'silent majority' of the United States?" No conclusions have been reached, but questions must continue and answers be sought.

But what are the comments submitted on this issue? A book could be written about them alone, for they are many and varied.

Most respondents who are not members of minority or ethnic groups write strongly that concern for all persons must be given high priority. A clergy group in the northeast says: "Of course this issue is of high priority! Minority groups are composed of human beings—of persons. Society and the church must always have an open ear to human cries. Better yet would be that all of us would make a genuine attempt to come to grips with human need before the cry is necessary. The Black Manifesto was a sad document to us. It reminded society of its failure to be human. It reminded the church of its failure to be the church—especially at the point of concern for one's fellowman!"

An executive women's group in the South Central Jurisdiction takes up the refrain. "If we take the gospel seriously," they say, "we *must* work for a society to come to pass in which all men and women may move with dignity, equality, and

57

freedom. The church must be in the lead challenging all of society by word and example to make decisions only after *full consideration* of what those decisions do *to people*. Wherever human beings are exploited and not allowed full humanity, the *church must cry out with them and for them*."

Conviction is strong in the responses from minority group members that "white racism" in society remains as one of the most urgent worldwide problems. Dr. Woodie White, of United Methodism's Commission on Religion and Race, speaks of white racism as being directed at black persons, brown persons, yellow persons, red persons. As a matter of fact, several from each of these ethnic groups quote Mr. White. In *Together* magazine he said: "White racism is not simply being antiblack or being a member of the White Citizens Council. It is often more subtle. . . . This may sound harsh but it is true: our society (Methodist families included) is developing 'little racists.' . . . Even at six, seven, and eight years of age, white children know that to be white is not only an advantage somehow, it is also to be innately of more value than are black, brown, red, or yellow people. The white youngster who calls middle-aged black people 'Mary' or 'John' instead of 'Mrs. Hill' or 'Mr. Jones' is being *taught* something about his worth in relationship to black adults. The white child who is told that his old clothes and toys will be given to 'underprivileged inner-city children' is being *taught* something about his worth in relationship to black children. The white, middle-class UMYFers who yearly make the 'go-see tour' in the inner city are simply having their racism reinforced." [1]

The following typical comments from ethnic minority groups show some of the intensity of their feelings.

The American Indian: "The American Indian has not been as vociferous recently as the black and the Spanish-American. Yet his plight has been as difficult for a longer time than theirs. Now, it is critical! The Indian is beating his war drum again: he is stirring his war paint. Will he have to use them again

[1] "White Racism and Your Family," *Together*, May, 1970.

58

to get his human rights? How about the church moving to respond before that happens rather than just reacting when it does? You know, Methodism has its reservations as does the nation."

The Spanish-American: "We, Hispanic-Americans, in the U.S.A. number now in excess of ten million. No less than seven million of us constitute a human disaster area. The rest of us, with few exceptions, represent for the perplexed American mainstream a resented case of arrested assimilation. . . . We come to this platform of the nation's conscience not so much to demand as to offer. . . . What can we expect from you right here and now?" [2] The "offer" is an invitation to "join us," the Spanish-Americans, in helping to secure basic human rights, education, training, justice, funds.

The Oriental-American: "An old Chinese proverb says, 'The wheel that squeaks gets greased.' The Oriental has settled back in philosophic silence long enough. We love the United States. That is why we are here. We appeal to be full citizens and to be full members of The United Methodist Church. Our youth are going to 'squeak' more. We hope that the church will listen and be concerned."

Many responses from whites indicate a reaction against confrontation tactics as a means of getting response from the white community. "They were needed and were effective in the past," says one group, "but they are now becoming counterproductive." Many are the expressions that screaming and pounding are no longer getting much mileage.

A bishop of The United Methodist Church states his feelings as follows: "I find myself increasingly hostile and alienated by the style of confrontation politics being employed by minorities. At first I was sympathetic. Now, as confrontation continues with all too little genuine working together resulting, I begin to fear that a reaction setting in among the whites

---

[2] From a speech by Jorge Lara-Brand, director of the Hispanic-American Institute, Austin, Texas.

may cause us to lose more than we have gained. I am moving to a personal position that the only long-range hope for society in this matter lies on the side of a style of open communication, followed by very specific and common goal setting in which all involved participate and to which both the dispossessed and the affluent can honestly give their energies. Confrontation got needed attention for a neglected issue. Further use of confrontation endangers gains already made. It is my opinion that minorities have gotten about all of the mileage out of screaming 'white racism' and disruption of meetings that they are going to get. We *must* find new ways of sensitizing persons to the needs that will keep them on board in working *with* minorities so that full human rights for all can be secured."

That bishop does not stand alone in his feeling. Hundreds of such comments were received.

Many comments urge strongly that persons in local areas be given the major responsibility for working out their own local problems. The national responsibility, however, is also recognized. Deep resentment is repeatedly voiced about national church staff moving into local areas to dictate paternalistically what their response to minorities should be. "We need stimulation, and we need to be prodded, but we also need to be involved in working out our own problems," writes a group in the southeast. Another annual conference in the south central region voices: "Of course response to ethnic groups must be a major concern of the country and the Methodist Church! However, response must be determined by those involved—both sides involved—not someone else from outside. Program simply cannot be determined any longer by some egotistical bureaucrat . . . sitting in a plush office . . . sensitizing himself to our sins but ignoring his own. Nothing has been more paternalistic than the programming of some national staff. Neither can needed response in human matters be determined by General Conference resolutions or national board pronouncements. We shall welcome any reasonable and intelligent views and suggestions. We shall be willing to sit down with our brothers to try to find Christian solutions to what have been, we admit, unchristian relationships. We shall not accept any further attempts by outsiders to determine and force solutions upon us. 'You can lead a horse to water, but you can't *make* him drink.' Any further attempts at determination *for us* will only result in alienation and will react to the detriment of connectional support for The United Methodist Church."

A large number of comments speak of the need of assuring equal rights for women (as distinct from the liberation movement). Interestingly, there are almost as many such expressions from men as there are from women. Many women speak of the need for equal rights in employment and for equal pay for the same work. Just as many, however, write with pride of the fact that "there is innate in woman the urge and drive to be a mother and a homemaker." They find repulsive, therefore, some of the Women's Liberation Movement approach. "Let woman be equal but feminine and proud of it," says one women's executive group.

And so we might go on, had we the space. It seems obvious that United Methodists see an urgent need to respond to minorities. They seem to feel that all that has gone before has been necessary, but they desire now to move out and find better ways of responsiveness.

A comment from Luke about the awakening of Peter dropped into the data:

He saw a rift in the sky, and a thing coming down that looked like a great sheet of sail-cloth. . . . In it he saw creatures of every kind, whatever walks or crawls or flies. Then there was a voice which said to him, "Up, Peter, kill and eat." But Peter said, "No, Lord, no: I have never eaten anything profane or unclean." The voice came again a second time: "It is not for you to call profane what God counts clean." . . . Peter began: "I now see how true it is that God has no favourites, but that in every nation the man who is godfearing and does what is right is acceptable to him." (Acts 10:11-16, 34-35 NEB)

61

2. World Peace and the Morality of War

During the period of intensive data gathering, depth of feeling has grown most rapidly on the issue of world peace and the morality of war. In fact, this issue has come close to supplanting minority concerns as the most urgent matter to be faced by society and the church. The two issues that follow in order of priority, the possible extinction of human life and the cheapness of human life today, are closely related to war and world peace. The intensity of feeling on those issues has also mushroomed.

Other denominations are finding the need for a similar priority on peace. The Board of Homeland Ministries of the United Church of Christ has announced "War and Peace" as its number one priority for immediate programming, and others are considering doing the same.

Comments emphatically decry violence in society today. Violence in Southeast Asia, violence in urban riots and campus confrontations, violence in the streets, violence on the highways, violence, with more subtle nuances, in man's treatment of his fellowman—all are thoughtfully treated.

Reactions to violence are varied, indicating that the denomination needs to give immediate guidance to the understanding of violence itself. Many simply want to avoid it. One black local church council on ministries in a north central city says, "We are moving our church to another location. It is no longer safe where we are." A white Administrative Board in a northeastern city has already done so: "Reluctantly, we have voted to close our church. No one dares attend evening meetings anymore. Members have been beaten and robbed in the church parking lot. We have lost count of those who have been threatened."

Not all, however, are fleeing. Many throw their weight behind dealing immediately with the social and economic factors giving rise to the violence. A western annual conference speaks for many others when they affirm: "The church must give immediate leadership to society in revamping the systems in our culture which result in the violence about us. We concur with Martin Luther King, Jr., who said, 'Passively to accept an unjust system is to cooperate with that system and thereby to become a participant of its evil.' We have all been passive and quiet too long. Let's clean our own 'temples' and give positive leadership to society *now!*"

Backlash against violence rears up again and again, often along with a request for "law and order." Hearings and comments from each of the five geographical regions confirm that many would agree with this statement from an annual conference summary in the northeast: "An urgent issue with which the church must deal is the *lack of respect for law and order.* The church must give leadership in bringing understanding to our people and must speak with a prophetic voice concerning the matter. A rightist reaction is now noted in our local churches and in our communities. This reaction approves more and more of law and order by force. Large numbers of persons are calling for it. People were stunned by what happened at Kent State; rather generally, they also approved of the appearance of the National Guard. At an annual conference meeting the next day a conference lay leader said, 'What else could they [the National Guard] do? We can't allow anarchy.' Most in attendance agreed. We are noting a rise in the number of those who would give up their own freedoms that order be maintained. They seem to have less fear of fascism than of rioting, violence on the streets, and chaos."

A large majority indicate immediate support for a loud and clear "peace offensive," as several student groups phrase it. Only a minority voice support for the war in Southeast Asia. Most advocate swift withdrawal of all fighting forces in that area and immediate transfer from "commitment to a military economy" to more "commitment to development of people at home and abroad rather than to their destruction." Indicative of many expressions is this from an annual conference summary in North Central: "The church needs to mount a counterforce to the military-industrial complex which controls half or more of our national budget. Too many lives have been

63

exploited and too many have been sacrificed in the name of fighting something or other. No one ever wins a war. Some get rich from it. We support loud speaking for peace by the church."

"Change world war to world development," says a women's group from a South Central summer school of missions. "Clean up our own backyards (that's difficult and uncomfortable) and also champion development for all peoples everywhere (it's easier to drum up support for something that is far off)," they continue.

A university professor comments on the difficulty of challenging the deeply entrenched military-industrial establishment in the United States. He is not certain, he says, that the average citizen who opposes the war and who cries for peace is aware of the trauma one will go through during the transition from a war economy to an economy aimed toward development. In the first place, we fight a powerful giant in challenging the military and its related industries. "Usually," he observes, "when you look for ivory, and find it, you discover that you also confront an angry elephant." Secondly, much military-related industry does not convert to "peaceful, humanitarian pursuits." During the long transition there will be unemployment, thousands of uprooted families, retraining to be done, etc. "When the average citizen gets caught in this trauma, it will take strong leadership from the church and from the government to keep a reaction from setting in."

Respondents who give strong support to a movement for peace and to immediate discussions of the morality of war also express sincere concern that "both sides of the question of morality" be carefully examined. Indications are that United Methodists are troubled in their thinking about "what is the moral responsibility of a strong nation to come to the aid of a weaker, brother nation being exploited, bullied, and invaded by an outside power." Another facet of troubled thinking is "the moral responsibility of a person to come to the aid of another person being attacked in the streets." "In our city," says a district group, "persons will not even allow their names to be used as witnesses when they have passively watched an attack on another person. They don't want to get involved."

Such comments can be summarized by the expression of an annual conference in the southeast: "Let us not, however, get this matter of moral responsibility out of perspective and out of total context. Any fool hates war! Any fool hates ever to be 'compelled' to intervention that could result in physical harm or death to himself. But let us look carefully at moral responsibility and the alternatives. Questions about the morality of war must be examined along with questions of the morality of permitting exploitation, enslavement, etc., of people anywhere —in Southeast Asia, the Middle East, down the block. Don't oversimplify the problem. It is a difficult one! Some of our leaders are becoming so enthralled with one side of the matter that they are in danger of ignoring the basic questions." This annual conference feels strongly enough that they sent this more fully stated version of a similar statement submitted at an earlier date.

All in all, opinions on this issue are intense and urgent. They include strong feelings about considering the whole scope of violence and about inclusion of at least two sides to the question of moral responsibility.

3. . . . for Tomorrow You May Die

The field instrument asked United Methodists to react to possible destruction of life by nuclear war, possible biological/ chemical blunders, possible poisoning of the environment, etc. Humanity lives today with a threat of extinction hanging over its head, a situation that gives rise to the "now generation" of our youth. "Eat, drink, and be merry, for tomorrow you may die."

Some comments say it is inappropriate for Christians even to care about such an issue. "Christians are charged with the responsibility to live the best they are able while they live—not worrying about a time they may be destroyed," states a local church study group. "Are you trying to be sensational?" asks a layman from the midwest.

Others, who would agree that Christians must do their best while they live, believe for that very reason that man must be concerned about the present use of knowledge, technology, and the environment.

A large majority of respondents commented under this issue on the "rape of the environment," to pick up an oft-mentioned phrase. Respondents feel that the matter of environment is so urgent that it must be considered in the context of possible extinction. A question appearing later in the field instrument dealt with environment as a facet of stewardship. This is totally rejected by a majority of participants as being too "innocuous" an approach. The reasoning of large numbers of such respondents is picked up in a summary from a large student group in the west: "Stewardship? Whose idea is it that all of a sudden environment is part of stewardship? How come no one thought of that before, while church members were getting rich raping the environment? It looks to us like the church is trying to get on the popularity bandwagon now that forces outside the church have finally begun to get a hearing on this matter! This matter is so urgent that nothing less than an all-out effort by all of society will make one damn bit of difference. Let the church throw what little influence it has left behind the all-out effort and not waste time trying to develop another largely irrelevant study about it while the matter gets worse. Don't fiddle while Rome burns."

The urgency expressed and the feeling that only government, prodded and supported by all, can get the environment cleaned up, are oft-repeated responses.

Comments about the "now generation" will be discussed in a section about youth in chapter 9.

4. Lost in the Shuffle

The paragraph stating the dimensions of this issue has to do with the population explosion, what happens to persons who are always crowded, the tendency in society to consider persons as unimportant, and man's proclivity to exploit and dehumanize his fellow humans.

More people register agreement with the statement of this issue than of any other—98.09 percent on the computer print-out. It would be difficult to obtain a higher consensus, even on the statement, "Man must eat to live."

Three groups give higher priority to this issue than to others. Persons over 55 years of age rate it second highest in their priorities of all issues; women and youth rate it somewhat higher than the average.

Many comments express consternation over the fact that professing Christians can turn a deaf ear to human cries around them; that some persons can nonchalantly stab, beat, and murder other humans with no pangs of conscience; that innocent men, women, and children are massacred in battle areas; that soldiers have been so dehumanized that they can jeer as they toss a "frag" [3] into a group of their buddies and then laugh as they walk away. So the comments go on. Hundreds of examples reported by participants point up the cheapness with which persons consider human life today.

Numerous groups of United Methodists are convinced that the church has a unique opportunity, and an urgent responsibility, to emphasize the importance of the *person*. A Northeastern annual conference puts it this way: "We are living in a time when individuals feel lost in the shuffle, more and more swallowed up by the crowd. The church should be concerned to pick them up as 'persons,' to help them to see that the individual is important to God and therefore to all in the fellowship. The church must emphasize personal importance and individual worth in all programming! Let's not fall victim to the rapidly spreading 'shotgun' approach which aims at the mass somehow hoping that it will help 'people.' The Christian

---

[3] The author's son, recently returned from Vietnam, says that a "frag" is a fragmentation grenade. Upon detonation it hurls metal fragments over an area, seriously injuring, maiming, or killing.

approach is personal in its valid spiritual and social ministries! Let's keep it that way."

Expressions from many sources indicate also that if the church is to know how to minister to persons, the congregation must get out "where persons live, and breathe, and work, and love, and cuss, and die," as a group of young married couples observe.

"*In the midst* of crowding, and all the rest, the church must be the church. It must get into the crowd and learn what it means to be crowded, and what it means to be lonely in the midst of chaotic hustle and bustle, and thus get a look at the points where the gospel might intersect such a situation. The church will not have anything to say in this situation from within its comfortable isolation. The church must get out and be crowded and quit retreating to its 'sanctuary' from it all," an urban missionary society reflects.

A South Central district group add their comment: "The church must be involved in total society and in the total needs of man. The church will need to go into the marketplace, the shop, the 'highways and byways.' The church can no longer expect people to come to it. A church willing to get its hands dirty, willing to smell pungent, acrid smells, willing to see the unlovely and to feel what living persons feel, is a must."

All agree that the church has allowed the "personal value and worth" of the individual to slip too near oblivion. That worth must be regained. "We shall know that we are on the way back," says an attorney, "when we can put our hand into that of an avowed communist, or maybe a Black Panther, and say, 'The God whom I worship loves you, and therefore so do I. You are invited into our fellowship.' "

5. Family Life and Sex Mores

The requests for resources on the issue of family life and sex mores are among the highest of those on all issues. Printed resources, audio-visuals, leadership training—you name the resource; people want it!

Little wonder! Customary family patterns and accepted sex mores are under heavy fire. Emerging new family living styles are openly advocated and practiced. With the advent of new contraceptive methods, premarital sex is being viewed differently—at least by those of the premarital generation.

John Wynn describes the problem thus: "Worried observers have been asking once again whether the family, as we know it, can survive its current problems. The question is not as far fetched as it appears, for the family is under heavy fire. Beset by massive changes across the world, the family's traditional provisions for faithful sexual relations in marriage and for responsible child-rearing in love are severely challenged by new developments that astonish even the best-informed and the most objective." [4]

Recognizing this situation, respondents raise all manner of questions. "Our pulpits are suddenly still. Now that most churches are giving more enthusiastic approval of mixed Christian marriages, how do we counsel our children about them?" ask young adults in Texas. "Now that we have the pill and pregnancy can be controlled, why is sex worse than a kiss?" asks a student group from the west. An older group inquires: "What does the church feel are the reasons for defending family patterns as we have known them? Or should they not be defended? A seminary teacher told us recently that family patterns of the recent past are those that grew up as part of the industrial revolution. 'Now that we are passing from the industrial revolution,' he said, 'family life patterns will also change.' What is to be found in biblical teachings and in biblical family life patterns that will help us to understand family life today?"

A large group voices great concern that family life and sex mores, like other vital issues, be dealt with in the light of the needs of persons. "We tend," say a group of young marrieds in the southeast, "to discuss the overall issue of family life and

[4] John Charles Wynn, "The American Family: Surviving Through Change," appearing simultaneously in *The Episcopalian*, *Presbyterian Life*, and *United Church Herald*, March, 1970.

sex without focusing on the problems of the persons involved in the matter. We feel that if boredom, loneliness, loss of intimacy, and sexual inadequacy are at the heart of the present breakdown in family form and sexual loyalty, as has been said, the church needs to deal quite specifically with such matters on a personal level. Let's stop moaning about the for-some-reason-or-the-other problem and get at the root causes—no matter what they are or where we need to come out."

Many would concur in the response that "this is no place for pronouncements. The matter cannot be improved by declaring positions!" "I agree that there is urgency in these matters of family life and sex mores but remain cynical as to the possibility of the church finding a useful consensus on beliefs and values relevant to the considering of them," observes one. "Help people think through their positions rather than drop positions from above," pleads the summary of one hearing group.

Significant numbers of respondents are "uptight" about changing attitudes toward sex. "There is too much permissiveness now!" says an annual conference in Southeastern. "The church has been too willing to allow *compromise* on basic values in family life and sex. We are too utterly ready to put our stamp of approval on every new idea in this matter, using the excuse that we must not be old-fashioned or that the pill has changed moral law," says another in South Central.

Recognizing such tension in the responses from within an annual conference in North Central, those who summarize attitudes for their people call for "honesty." "Nothing is more disturbing to our church members than the changing outlook on sex. The new permissiveness and freedom is not understood or accepted. Why not an honest facing of the matter—especially with adults. (Our youth are quite open and honest.) Adults are still largely responsible for sex counseling with their children—at least until the kids discover that parents are not open. Face the issue of sex honestly and openly. We must not avoid the subject because large numbers of our people still feel that talking about it is somehow not quite nice!"

And so, we come back to where we started. Very high is the request for resources—leadership training, audio-visuals, materials. Very low is the response to resolutions and pronouncements. And one other thing, reflects an annual conference in the southeast: "It would be helpful if workshop leaders could speak from actual day-to-day involvement in family problems and sexual tensions. We, too, read books. We need 'rap sessions' with others involved in the daily tensions on this one."

6

ISSUES: THROUGH STAINED GLASS DARKLY

Assuming that you have a normal pulse beat, it will not quite keep up with the increase in world population. . . . Every time your pulse throbs, the population of the world will have added more than one human being. —William Vogt, "People!"

Although the issues considered in this chapter are given lower priority in the feelings and attitudes of United Methodists, the expressions on them have important implications in the designing of denominational program. Let's take a quick glance at such issues. "Sometimes the expressions on issues given lower priority," says one bishop who conducts listening posts, "are just as clearly indicators of the needs of United Methodists as are those on high priority concerns."

6. Polarization in Society

"Polarized? Not us with you! The church isn't important enough for us to be polarized with it. You just don't matter anymore. But remember, that's the way you chose for it to be." These words from a black caucus in a large western city are, in a way, describing polarization while at the same time denying it. In doing so they are responding to a dimension of the issue stated in the field instrument: "Many who formerly felt that the church was important now feel that it is totally irrelevant." The rest of the response indicates that the respondents had been moved to that conclusion by denominational promises not kept, by resolutions without action, by "paternalistic, band-aid church approaches."

Respondents were also asked to comment on the polarizations between those of differing viewpoints, between those of differing theologies, and between the church and the secular world. Much of what they say is included in the consideration of other trends, issues, and church needs. But the intensity of feelings is the vital point here.

The largest number of comments say that the church must be big enough to claim persons and groups of differing positions. Consensus and "watered-down, lowest denominator agreement" are no good—nor are they possible in a society changing as rapidly as ours, say many. Repeatedly, comments urge the denomination to make differences authentic; to keep those who differ in communication with each other and thus learning from each other; and to be ever alert to the fact that the Bible and history often bring us "fresh glimpses of God's revelation" in expressions far different from "the then institutionalized positions." "Vitality and renewal might result from a Christian cross-pollinization of such different positions in The United Methodist Church. History reminds us that the whole truth spans time, issues, and viewpoints." So speaks an annual conference summary from the northeast.

The large response points up another facet: many are irritated that anyone thinks the church irrelevant today. Some are riled, it would seem, because their home communities remain insulated from the rapid change and tensions affecting others. Another group of respondents seem nettled to think that their congregation might be considered unimportant and irrelevant. They sincerely feel that their fellowship is sensitive, responsive, and relevant. A typical exasperated expression comes from a large urban local church Council on Youth Ministries in North Central: "Who feels that the church is irrelevant— national church leadership? That must be it, because no one feels that way around our congregation! Our members are so busily involved in 'being Christian' that they do not waste time forming discussion groups on the discussion of 'the irrelevancies of relevancy.' We leave that to national staff who seem to have lots of time these days to discuss the irrelevancies of someone else. So they end up making the local church the whipping boy. (It's always more comfortable to discuss someone else's irrelevancies and someone else's 'oughts' than it is to discuss our own.) Maybe denominational bureaucrats 'ought' to get off their office chairs and get involved in a moving church such as ours—or get involved in one that is not moving and help it to be so. The only polarization, that we sense to be alarming, is that between local church members and national leadership who sit around and scream polarization while doing nothing in a local church or in a local community."

Students from many sections of the United States talk about what they believe are the solutions for polarizations between the church and society. "Reorder priorities, especially financial commitments," they say, and "get out in the world and get with it." A group of graduate students at Indiana University add their voice: "Society does not long stay polarized with institutions which serve persons rather than self. Society will not long remain polarized with the church if it will commit its resources to 'beautiful personhood' rather than to 'beautiful buildings.' Let the church turn from her now recognized 'altars' and look for responsible service opportunities to persons around the cathedrals. There is the altar where God is to be found! Damn the shingles! Let the roof leak! Fewer and fewer are coming into the building anyway."

So the irritations and aggravations come in reaction to polarization. Most place the issue rather low in their list of priorities, feeling that "this issue will be cared for if we adequately deal with the high priorities." Only one age group observes that polarization itself should be of high priority; the age group 45 through 54 places it number two on their list. This fact may imply that this group feels most polarized by all that is happening in society today.

7. Environment: Act or Die

Those commenting on environment are quite clear that the issue must be dealt with as a "crisis," and most gave it priority under the issue of living in a time of possible total extinction of human life. Respondents are suspicious that any attempt to deal with environment in the category of stewardship will be innocuous and ineffective. "Just like the church to try to throw a little hay in the trough after the horse has gotten out!" remarks a South Central annual conference lay meeting.

In spite of the feeling of crisis about the environment, it is evident that those who wrote comments experience great difficulty in changing from the viewpoint that mankind is in competition with nature and must conquer it, to a viewpoint that sees nature as something to be conserved, with which people must cooperate. Little understanding is expressed of how all, collectively and individually, have a responsibility to prevent the planet's soil, water, and air from being contaminated lethally.

People see the urgency—but mostly for someone else! Respondents have read the projections that, at the rate imbalance is developing, some scientists place the life expectancy of the human race at just twenty-five years—and that optimists in the field say one hundred years. Comments see the possibility of world starvation as well as the threat of humans poisoning themselves with their own waste products, especially in industrialized countries.

"Act or die!" cries a group of college students. "Now!" echoes another. "Band-aids can't solve the world's ecological problems," says Dr. Richard Baer, Jr., of Earlham College. He then commends a continually deepening church involvement pegged on action and pressure on local, state, and federal political units.

The summary of a wide sampling in the northeast pulls together the thinking on this issue. "The church is not to jump on every bandwagon of need that is rolling by in our world— especially this one—if by jumping on, we mean to discuss it some more. By the time the church gets to what we ought to do, we will all be dead from pollution and abuse. Government is the only place where action can be mounted quickly enough on this issue. Let's direct our efforts toward the challenging of government to do something *now!* It is only there that we find resources and power structures adequate for the facing of the environmental crisis. We may not know all that there is to be known; study might help that. But, we know enough already to scream. So, *scream!*"

Some respondents express fears that the present interest in ecology and environment may "degenerate into faddism distracting interest from the main issues—maybe even add to the problem." Such expressions pick up the note struck by Alan Ternes: "Saving the world," he says, "has become big business. Ecology has exploded like an oil boom, spawning a deluge of promoters hustling everything from exhaust arresters and water purifiers to mammoth fund-raising campaigns. . . . Forests are cut down to furnish paper for [ecological] books, magazines, newsletters and fund-literature. As Paul Erlich, leading doomsday prophet of population growth, is reported to have said, 'If you are traveling on the *Titanic,* you might as well go first-class.' Everybody seems to be clamoring to get on board." [1] Participants feel a danger that the crisis of the environment may get sidetracked by "faddism," and they do not want their denomination to become a part of that problem. "Let nothing sidetrack the church from loudly thrusting her influence into the battle—not even interesting studies," says a United Methodist whose career is to work on the issue. Many concur.

8. The Message, not the Medium

Participants were asked to respond to the concepts that the old symbolic language of the church no longer communicates the gospel to contemporary man; communication has broken down between the church and the world, therefore,

[1] Ternes, "Who's Saving What?" *True,* December, 1970, p. 32.

and the church must immediately seek new symbols that will better communicate the gospel in the new culture of today.

Resistance to these ideas runs very high. United Methodists agree the least on this issue of all those to which they reacted.

Most comments, even from those of differing theological and sociological viewpoints, indicate a feeling that "the old symbolic language still communicates." The general consensus is that the breakdown in communications is due more to a "crisis of confidence" with the church than to any defect in the symbols.

An annual conference summary in South Central brings together the attitudes and feelings, expressed by others in different ways, of thousands of responses: "We are overly concerned in our striving to find new 'words' and new 'thought-forms' to use in communicating with secular man. Secular man is intelligent enough to understand ancient and symbolic language whenever he feels that it may communicate something vital, something that matters, to him. Our greater concern should be with the evident feeling of secular man that what the church is trying to communicate to him really doesn't matter. Changing words and thought-forms will not communicate to the receiver what he feels to be unimportant. Let us spend our time and energy on the question, 'Why does secular man find the message of the church unimportant today?' Such a consideration might put us all under conviction (to use an old thought-form) in a way that just might result in something vital and creative."

Another summary of a wide sampling in a western annual conference concurs: " 'Bad communication' is the new bag into which we bundle our excuses for failure. Did it ever occur to the denomination that we may be trying to communicate something that no one wants to hear anymore—'isolated,' 'irrelevant,' 'Sunday school religionism'? If the message is not relevant to life, no one will listen whatever the symbol. Our conference wants more attention given to *what* we are trying to communicate than to *how*. Our *how* is not that bad."

There is definitely, however, a sizable interest in the use of new forms and symbols for communicating Christian meaning and truth. Expressions from youth are very appreciative of the use of banners, posters, etc. Almost all youth comments make it clear that new symbols, such as the contemporary peace symbol, and new music communicate with them better than the older ways. A college group comments: "Banners, posters, and even writings on buildings seem to be the new way of getting things across. The church ought to use them—especially since denominational publications can't communicate. (They're not, you know!) Youth will show the church how, through use of symbols, to get the message across—to the world *and* to the church."

Respondents are saying, then, two things. First, they feel that the church will be able to communicate with the world only when the world can find relevance and importance in the message. "Tinkered-with symbols and thought-forms" will not be any more effective than those already at hand. The message is the point.

Secondly, many feel that when new symbols and thought-forms communicate, use them. John Wesley did. The old is not sacred because it is old.

9. Less Work, More Leisure?

Reacting to statements about machines replacing men in industry, decreasing need for man's work as fewer workers are able to produce all needed goods, and the predicted rise in leisure time, respondents show high resistance. A large majority of comments express shock and antagonism. Only males seem to understand and to accept the growing effect of automation on life, placing this issue second among their priorities.

One comment in the field instrument that triggers widespread resistance is: "It is predicted that less than 20 percent of the work force will soon produce all of the goods needed by society." Such a statement seems rather conservative in the light of Don Fabun's observation: "Within less than a generation in the United States two percent of the population may be able to produce all the food and manufactured goods required by the other 98 percent." [2]

Nevertheless, United Methodist respondents express shock and rejection that this will occur. Their reaction bears out a prediction by Leo Cherne in *Nation's Business:* "In a sense, when work is reduced, as it almost certainly will be, there is a very real crisis of values for people generally. Great groups of people have been trained by nothing in their whole culture, background, religion and philosophic conceptions, for anything other than work as a meaningful activity."

Hundreds of reactions were received. From a large lay group in the southeast: "We do not believe that 20 percent of the work force will ever produce all of the goods." "I resist even the thought of not having meaningful work," cries an annual conference lay leader. "This will never happen! Most of the people that we know would be miserable without productive work," chimes in a group of clergy from the west. "Hogwash," writes an Iowa hog farmer. "It would be awful if that happened." "You must be kidding." "That isn't so"—the replies go on.

Respondents react more positively to a predicted rise in available leisure time. Large numbers ask that the church begin planning for such a contingency. "More leisure, or discretionary time as some call it, gives the church a wonderful opportunity to cultivate service," says a North Central group. But, write many others, "The church will not be able to claim our growing leisure time unless it comes up with more relevant, exciting reasons for doing so than it has in the past."

Some comment that the concept of leisure time is largely a myth. Observations from this group can be condensed into another of Fabun's statements. "Free-time," he says, "is figured negatively by deducting subsistence, work and commuting time from the work year. It is customarily referred to as 'leisure

[2] Fabun, *The Dynamics of Change*, p. I-20.

79

time,' but it is anything but leisure. We use it up shopping, calling on friends or relatives, reading, watching TV, going to church or the theater, etc. As free-time increases because of shorter working hours, the new increment of time is largely used for chores around the house, repairs, remodeling or gardening. In our times, free-time is anything but free." [3] The result, say many respondents, is that such time is immediately gobbled up in other activities; it is not lying around waiting for someone to pick it up and put it to use.

Indications are that United Methodists need to put more thought into the relationships between work and play and between work and income. The comments seem to deal quite hazily with what is a meaningful use of time. Respondents do not for the most part seem concerned that the church include the subject in church programming.

10. The Biomedical Revolution

Participants, by and large, are not caught up in the moral and ethical issues of human organ transplants, possible genetic control of man, and artificial insemination—all matters to which they are invited to react. Neither do those who replied seem greatly worried about the possibility of biomedical practices raising difficult questions of the meaning of life and death or the meaning of the individual. "Will such biomedical practices make it more difficult to answer the question, 'Who am I?'" was asked. Most do not think it will.

A majority have strong feelings in one regard, however. "If this matter does become a problem," pleads an executive women's group, "don't try to solve it by resolutions or pronouncements. In that eventuality give guidance, and train our ministers to be counselors, to help us think the matter through. Such decisions are primarily personal." A summary statement from a South Central annual conference speaks for many: "This is not a place where more board pronouncements are needed! This is an area where clergy need training in pointing

[3] *Ibid.*, p. V-7.

individuals toward making the best decision in a specific situation. Individual decision-making is the crux of this matter. Pronouncements only irritate—especially from those not even facing such decisions." "Resources, not a big news release!" adds another group.

The last observation brings out an urgent need from respondents. The data show more requests for resources on this issue than on any other mentioned. A Northeastern annual conference summary says: "Since this matter deals primarily with personal, ethical decision-making, the local church, its pastor and its laymen, should be provided with resources to establish a strong foundation upon which to stand in the making of such decisions. Of course we need to be aware of possibilities for the total church to speak out on such issues *but only* if this speaking out is the outgrowth of local response. Let's lead the local church member to understand and respond to biomedical matters. Then, the church as a body will better know what to say about them. Pronouncements from ivory towers need wider participation in formulation."

Requests for assistance in thinking through the moral and ethical issues of biomedical developments come most urgently from those who are forced to respond to them right now. "My doctor wants me to receive an organ transplant as soon as possible. Is it right?" asks one woman. We put her in touch with a counselor who we think can help.

One of the field instruments ended up at a meeting of a medical association of a large North Central city. The doctor who took it there asked if the members felt the church should be giving guidance on such matters. The summary from the group, received in semi-legible, prescription script, tells what happened:

"Our medical association (interfaith) was stimulated and intrigued by the field instrument to the place that we invited church and university leaders to come to our next meeting to discuss several of the issues with us. We enthusiastically endorse what you are doing. . . . Especially, however, we endorse

81

giving attention to matters in the biomedical field. As physicians, we need dialogue with churchmen concerning moral and ethical factors in the decisions that must be made (i.e. organ transplants). We need help! But, so do our patients at such times! We encourage the church to proceed in helping persons to make the best decisions in such matters. At present we all seem to be caught flat-footed and open-mouthed. It would seem to be impossible for the church, or anyone else, to reach one position that will fit all cases. It will be most helpful, however, for the church to give leadership that will help those involved to reach the best possible decision!"

Another such group wraps up a similar comment by saying: "It will be helpful if the church can provide the kind of experts who can speak with doctors and enable them to think through the many ethical issues related to life and death and the health and welfare of man."

It is clear, is it not, that the church must seriously weigh responsibility for dealing with the moral and ethical issues of potentially explosive biomedical practices. Church members, for the most part, feel little urgency. Patients and physicians feel great urgency!

One other facet comes out in responses on this issue. Youth tend to shy away from the church's dealing with the biomedical matters "because the church will make them too muddy and complicated, you know." Young people tend to approve of what is being done biomedically and to be satisfied merely to ask the question, "Does it make for a better and more beautiful life for someone? If so, man, do it!" Most youth respondents do not feel that it will be helpful to deal with such matters philosophically and theologically, except perhaps for "tired old men." This impatience with academic discussion is seen in the following comment from a young man in a northeast urban area. Although the response is a personal one, it is included in a larger youth summary with the comment, "This speaks for all of us." The reader may not approve of all the language, but the meaning is clear.

"I'm sick of 'Who am I?' In my church I'm told I'm some

kind of a spiritual something, but it is never related to reality in the world in which I live. The world they talk about, I don't see! I'm a man with hurting guts—you know what I mean? When will the church have something to say about how to keep my guts from falling apart? In my church I'm tempted to jump up occasionally and yell Bullshit! ! ! The church wants to speculate in some ethereal realm about who I am. Hell, I'm not *there*. I'm *here*, man! I'm flesh and bones that will be faced with some of the decisions you list. . . . And, I'm not expecting much help from the church in making those kinds of gutsy decisions. They'll still be talking about it."

Add to this a cry of a youth at a Miami hearing: "I don't want to hear any more sermons about heaven! Heaven can wait! I want help now on how to live each day as I face choices about drugs, sex, career, marriage. I could care less about heaven."

7
NEEDS: OPEN THE DOORS
AND SEE ALL THE PEOPLE

> And so the Church will change or not, depending on
> the blowing of the wind. . . . The Church will move
> as Jesus did or cling to what it can't sustain. Authorita-
> tive frowns of yesteryear may mellow into embarrassed
> grins of those who dimly sense their business is to
> please old ghosts, or not, depending on the blowing
> of the wind.
> —Stephen Rose, *The Grass Roots Church*

United Methodists had a great deal to say on the specifically
"churchy" needs of the denomination, not only in reaction to
those listed on the field instrument but in a great many spontaneous opinions on other needs.

The nine factors named on the field instrument are, in
order of weighted priority:

1. More lay involvement at all levels.
2. The crisis in the ministry.
3. Rethinking the meaning of commitment.
4. The need for clear communication.
5. More opportunities to designate funds.
6. Rethinking of theology and values.
7. Developing new forms of ministry.
8. Finding more workable church organizational forms.
9. Renewing the connectional system.

This chapter will discuss the top five priorities under church
needs, and chapter 8 will look at the next four. Because re-

spondents name more additional needs in this area than any other, spontaneous comments are dealt with in chapter 9. Such needs include ecumenicity, church school curriculum, youth, national church pronouncements, emerging new styles of operation, preaching, and "meaningless words and phrases from which we have gotten all of the mileage we are going to get." First, however, let's examine the top five priorities.

1. Let's Get Involved

Recent years have seen the rise in the United States of various groups concerned about the "quality" of American life. For some, interest centers on the kids' schools and who attends them. Law and order "grabs" others. All kinds of issues become focal points—job security, the military-industrial complex, the right to "do your own thing," and tricky questions like sex, prayer in the schools, drugs, student unrest, long hair on boys and short skirts on girls. In commenting on the surge of such groups, Tom Wicker, *The New York Times* political analyst, says that "the one thing that most nearly unites them is the apprehensive and angry conviction that the individual citizen cannot make his voice heard, his presence felt, his views heeded, in 20th Century America."

It seems to be "most nearly" the same feeling that unites the United Methodists who participate in this sample. With 1 being the heaviest weight that could be given to any of the needs on a scale of 9 up to 1, the priority of more lay involvement was weighted 1.29. There was no significant departure from this figure by any comparison group in the computer print-outs, though a few national board staff gave it lower priority.

The level of agreement was only slightly lower. The paragraph in the field instrument speaks of the fact that laymen demand more participation in the formulation of denominational pronouncements, in decision-making at all levels of denominational life, and in designing program for their own local situation and for the world. Weighted values on agreement come out at 1.39, highest agreement on any of the needs.

Many denominations report that some of their major administrative problems today hinge on poor performance by those who feel uninvolved, cooperation withheld by members for many reasons, high turnover in membership, and the need for extra recruiting and training. Respondents in this sample appear to feel that lay participation, or the lack of it, lies at the heart of all these matters.

The demand for involvement is not peculiar to the churches. The business environment section of General Electric, for instance, has for some years explored trends in the business world. In the latest reevaluation of their findings, General Electric makes some observations about institutional and organizational changes in the next ten years. One of those seems to be bolstered by the response of United Methodists. Let's look at it.

"All organizations will be operated less and less by the dictates of administrative convenience, more and more to meet the wants and aspirations of their membership," is a main heading in the General Electric report. "So long as organizations were concerned principally with a relatively stable environment and the maintenance of internal order, they could rely on the routine administration of detailed procedures (the great strength of bureaucratic systems). Dealing with the uncertainty of change reduces the value of set procedures, and increases the value of individual initiative. . . . Managers (of *any* organization) must expect that considerations of individual motivation, group relationships and personnel costs (including the 'hidden' costs of poor performance, withheld cooperation, high turnover and extra recruiting and training) will weigh much more heavily in their decision-making in the future." [1]

United Methodist laity are tired of being "in but not of" the church. They demand more involvement in basic decision-making and threaten to use the "vote of their dollar" to get it.

[1] Ian H. Wilson, "How Our Values Are Changing," *The Futurist*, February, 1970, p. 5.

Groups within the church who feel uninvolved demand participation in working out their own destinies. "We are weary," they say, "of being planned *for!*" "Do not plan for us separately," is the growing crescendo from ethnic groups, women, and youth, "but involve *us* and our *concerns* in the overall planning of United Methodism!"

This ground swell of feeling was driven home to the general Program Council at a meeting in the fall of 1970 when tentative priorities, in response to these data, were being considered for the 1970s. When a separate section on planning for youth was suggested, the youth who were present immediately and vigorously objected. "Youth do not want to be treated separately," they reacted. "Youth want to be part of the whole. Youth have the impression that the denomination wants to deal with 'our' problems, because that is more comfortable than dealing with 'your' problems. Let youth be an authentic participant along with all others! Then, let us together deal with 'Our' problems spelled with a capital O—meaning the common concerns of us all." [2]

The data clearly show that before the best participation can take place, techniques must be developed. Many an older clergyman, for instance, feels more comfortable speaking "to" people than working "with" them. His training was based on "get out there and tell people what the gospel demands of them." (Some would maintain that the young seminarian today is just as prone to this approach.) Many older clergymen feel ill at ease in situations where answers must be developed by the group of committed Christians instead of coming primarily from him. Many a younger clergyman, who is looking for participation and is alerted to the necessity for immediate relevancy in the church, is "turned off" by the lethargy of his members and their deadening preoccupation with institutional maintenance. Many a layman and laywoman, also unaccus-

[2] Transcribed from a statement by a youth member of United Methodism's national Program Council at Syracuse, New York, September, 1970.

tomed to authentic participation, will need to develop the skills of participation.

Yet the data are definitely not demanding the kind of participation that "waters everything down to the lowest common denominator." Rather, they show awareness of, and rejection of, such a concept while at the same time demanding the "right for responsible involvement"—even though decisions may move against some participants.

A very small minority of respondents see no value in wide participation in planning process and in decision-making. This is only to be expected, according to many writers on the subject. James Wilson, associate professor of government at Harvard, writes that "not everyone has the same taste for collegial decision-making and the opportunity it supposedly affords for cooperation, problem-solving, and 'self-actualization.' Some persons have a taste for routine, deference, power, and certainty or a desire to reserve for nonorganizational settings their self-expression." [8]

A majority, however, see great values in developing participation in the church. James Clark, of the University of California's Graduate School of Business, writes about the widely known Hawthorne studies by Western Electric Company. Administrators at Western Electric invited workers from the assembly lines to meet with them regularly and help discover the determining factors in productivity. Administrators followed the workers' suggestions by changing work schedules, intensity of lighting, and other factors. The interesting result was this: No matter what they did—turn the lights up, turn the lights down, lengthen the work day, shorten the work day, lengthen the rest periods, shorten the rest periods—productivity kept going up and up.

Thus was discovered the "Hawthorne Effect." It does not mean that no matter what you do to people, if you bring in a bunch of researchers and put them into the same room, produc-

---

[8] Wilson, "Innovation in Organization: Notes Toward a Theory," in *Approaches to Organizational Design*, ed. by James D. Thompson (Pittsburgh: University of Pittsburgh Press, 1966), p. 213.

tivity will go up. Rather, says Mr. Clark, it means that if you *listen* to people, get their feelings and advice, you intensify *meaning* for these people. Meaning and work are inseparable. If you listen to people, treat them as persons and their opinions as important, get their feelings and suggestions, they tend to find more *joy* in their work. They feel involved. They feel then that they are doing something for *themselves* and *not just for you.*

Thousands of written comments are the basis for this analysis of the need for more lay participation. Let us quickly look at a few typical comments out of the vast blizzard of expression.

The value of authentic participation in stimulating inactive but far from apathetic laymen is voiced in several ways. Many see participation as "motivation." An annual conference summary from North Central states it for most: "Motivation of the laity is an absolute must! Otherwise denominational leadership will find themselves commanding a battle with no troops or firing a locomotive 'running wild' down the right track but with nothing following. Such motivation can best come by authentic involvement of the laity, sincerely and realistically, at all levels of decision-making. The Program Council concept is an excellent way to get such involvement going if we would let it work *and* if we would set meetings for the convenience of laity rather than for the convenience of clergy. Do what has to be done to get the laity participating! When the lay person begins to feel that he or she is really wanted, that his or her feelings and opinions will make a difference, he or she will be willing not only to participate but also to support that which results. Without authentic participation the church will quickly die."

From an annual conference in the southeast comes this one: "Lay involvement is the only thing that has a possibility within it of snapping the church out of its slump. To get lay involvement, we shall first need to overcome a 'crisis of confidence,' a matter much voiced in our hearings. Laymen don't really believe that we want their participation. They do not believe that such involvement will make any difference. 'We have been asked for opinion before,' voiced the laymen of one local church, 'only to discover that decisions had already been made as to what program would be followed.' Other laity are speaking as though they feel that it is already too late for participation to be meaningful: 'The church is relatively out of it!' they say. Secondly, to get lay involvement it is felt that we shall need to give at least as much consideration to laity as we do to clergy in the setting of the times and places of meetings. And another thing, only have such meetings when important matters are to be considered. Meetings must be on important matters *that have not been decided already*. Laity sense hidden agendas and rubber-stamping procedures very quickly. Yes, lay involvement! But, make it real!" An overwhelming number of comments indicate a feeling that ministers go to meetings just to go to meetings and to avoid more important matters at home.

Large numbers of comments say that more implementation results from wider participation in planning and design of program. "If local persons are not involved in the planning, they will no longer buy the program or emphasis—no matter how good it may be. Otherwise, we are just going through motions (or passing resolutions) with nothing *really* happening," says an annual conference in the southeast. "The present Quadrennial Emphasis[4] is the best example," they continue. "It was brilliantly conceived but only by a few 'up there.' Nothing much has happened but a little money and what a little money can do. We hope that no one really thinks that anything much has happened in the local church; they do not even understand what is being funded. We missed the boat! Why didn't we involve persons at every level in designing such an important and needed emphasis? The program would have

[4] United Methodism's present Quadrennial Emphasis, a priority emphasis of the denomination for the years 1968-1972, is called "The Fund for Reconciliation." It proposes to raise twenty million dollars to fund projects and programs of a reconciling nature. To date, the emphasis is falling short of its goals.

started more slowly with such participation, but more would have resulted in the final analysis. This should be a lesson for the church. When the design is frozen, so is the emphasis. No one is buying bureaucratically and paternalistically designed ideas of 'what those poor, stupid souls out there ought to be doing.'"

Before anyone is exasperated enough by such grass-roots expression as this to retort, "But we have representative participation now in The United Methodist Church," let's take a look at the way members see this.

One annual conference summary, with which the conference Program Council and staff concur, observes: "If laity were involved in plans before 'packages' were announced or pronouncements made, there would more likely be implementation and acceptance. And, this involvement means *any* layman who is interested. It does not mean the lip service to lay involvement that pertains when only a few are present. If the church cannot take the time for real lay involvement from the grass roots up, then don't even talk about it. Everyone knows that the usual lay involvement in the national boards is innocuous and not really representative at all." This feeling about present lay representation on national boards, expressed in the southeast, is echoed throughout the denomination.

A person from another geographical area, who identifies himself as a member of one of the denomination's largest national boards, the Board of Missions, is even more pointed: "Actions of the general board to which I belong are about as representative of The United Methodist Church as are the actions of our city council—its members are all Methodist, too. Our general board membership breaks down into divisional membership for the 'gut' sessions of business. Actions are taken in the divisions with few laity present and are then rubber-stamped by the total board. By the time the total board meets, everyone is either ignorant about the details of what is recommended or too tired to go into it all again. At one of our recent meetings I chanced to overhear one of the board's general secretaries say that he needed only eighteen votes, clergy and laity, to get anything through that he wanted. Yet the same man defended one of his pet projects at our annual conference by saying, 'This is the action of the Board of Missions!' This is representation? Such unrepresentative actions will not be accepted any longer, and I will not defend them in the conference that I represent."

Clearly, then, United Methodist participants see more lay involvement at all levels of the denomination as their crucial need. Just how this can best be done, making laity involvement and stimulation by leadership authentic, will be a major issue in the future.

2. The Crisis in the Ministry

Reactions to the question on crisis in the ministry indicate the only major disagreement between clergy and laity in the entire sample, not about priority but about root causes.

The field instrument stated such dimensions of the crisis as ministers leaving the ministry, fewer young men entering the ministry than in the past, older and younger ministers openly disagreeing on valid approaches to ministry, and the lethargy of laymen as a strong contributing factor to the problem.

Agreement with these dimensions ran high—97.85 percent. "One can hardly get that high an agreement even on motherhood," one researcher commented. The written comments, however, indicate that the agreement between laity and clergy stops right there. Let's let some comments from each group speak for themselves.

From one of the largest annual conference pastors' schools in North Central comes the following: "A major part of the crisis, which is real and urgent, is the stifling of creativity of the minister. Ministers who want to be creative, innovative, and contemporary (or even those who just want to be a shepherd to their people) find that they are 'boxed in' by the system of United Methodism. First, there is the enigma of the local church. Too often it is apathetic to urgent local problems demanding Christian involvement. Many members are re-actionary to the point of seeing any new proposal as 'Commu-nistic'—only old ways, even though some of the 'old' ways are not as old as the century, are American and Christian. Mem-bers want to do the same old thing in the same old way. They react as though it is heresy to study at any time other than Sunday morning. To worship at any other time would be un-thinkable—even for those who want to. Then, there is the even more dehumanizing cabinet, bishop, conference staff, etc., who expect the minister to do certain things—many certain things—and to report with three certified copies to the district and conference offices. By the time a minister gets through with what is expected of him, the poor guy hardly has time to eat his dinner. A minister's dedication to Christ is more often measured by his response to the hierarchy than by any other norm. We could go on to bigger boxes, but just let us say, 'Free the clergy to minister!' When the minister feels that he is not boxed in, most of the crisis will disappear. Challenge local churches to respond to creative leadership and to try new ways with old truth. Challenge 'the system' to free the clergy for innovative, creative ministry. Encourage ministers to try, even' if they fail, in which case encourage them to have an-other go at it. Until the clergy, especially those young enough to still get out, feel authentic freedom, you will still have a crisis in the ministry."

Laity, however, see the reasons for the crisis in another area altogether. The lay response indicates that the crisis rests upon "lack of commitment." Here are five comments, one from a lay group summary in each jurisdiction.

"Ministers lack commitment! They would rather run to meetings, meetings, meetings, than do their job. If meetings could bring in the kingdom of God, we would be supporting the space program, because we would need new worlds to con-vert. Ministers blame meetings 'demanded of them' for not working at what the gospel says should be their primary task, to 'preach the gospel to every creature.' Laymen are not that naïve."

93

"We are sick of uncommitted, fearful clergymen. No wonder we have uncommitted, fearful laymen! The sheep follow the shepherd."

"Lethargic laymen have been inspired by lethargic clergymen."

"If The United Methodist Church ever again emphasizes 'the call to preach,' the crisis will soon be over. Too many of our ministers are recruited—not called. Therefore, when ministers run into their first opposition, they drop out. *And*, our recruitment policies are so shoddy that any business using them would go bankrupt. They would have a crisis, too."

"Could our recruitment policies be the problem? We are hearing it said that almost anything is a call to preach—from an upset stomach to draft dodging. As easy as it is to become a clergyman, we are surprised that the Mafia hasn't seized upon it as a good place to practice their ministry!"

Not one lay comment sees the crisis in the same context as do ministers; not one ministerial comment sees the crisis in the same context as do the laity.

A constructive suggestion made in large numbers of clergy comments is that the "sabbatical year for study be made a reasonable expectation rather than a rosy, impracticable paragraph in the *Discipline*." [5] For years, respondents complain, the idea of a sabbatical year has been listed. It is not used, they feel, because:

"No provision is made for pay. A minister with a family cannot afford to go on sabbatical without visible means of support. Few ministers are able to save for such a contingency on present ministerial salaries."

"Few ministers would take the chance. If you leave a Methodist conference to go on sabbatical, you are 'out,' with the distinct possibility that you may have to start at the bottom again upon your return. Who's going to do that? Present

---

[5] United Methodism's *Book of Discipline* makes provision for a sabbatical leave for ministers, after ten years' service, for "travel, study, rest or other justifiable reasons." No provision is made, however, for pay or for maintaining seniority in the system.

policy seems to support the one who stays ignorant but on the job. My district superintendent counsels his ministers not to even consider a sabbatical."

Ministerial respondents believe sabbatical leave will help deal with the crisis in the ministry by making it possible for ministers to engage in continuing education on a reasonable basis. The same ministers refer to present programs of continuing education as "innocuous and most often designed just to make the participant a nicer member of the system." Respondents express feelings that sabbaticals can easily be made effective if the denominational leadership wants them to be.

One creative suggestion that offers a way of making the sabbatical workable says: "Grant a minister a sabbatical leave from the church that he serves, with their permission, with the understanding that he will return to the same pastorate for at least one year. That takes care of seniority. Have several ministerial members available, with base salary paid by the conference, to move into the parsonage and substitute for that minister. Let the minister on sabbatical continue to draw his base salary. That takes care of income. Give any expense account at the church in question to the substituting minister. There are retired ministers in almost every conference who would willingly and effectively serve. Churches with multiple staff will have no problem."

Sabbatical leave, however, is only one facet of possible continuing education that receives wide attention. Other suggestions are also made, most of which fall into two pigeonholes:

1. The development of lay-clergy academies where together laymen and clergymen can engage in continuing education. A large number of respondents suggest developing these in local areas "with resource persons being brought in by cable television to many points at once." Dialogue can then continue under local leadership. Others suggest converting one or more seminaries into lay-clergy academies with "intense courses of short duration." A common note runs through all the ideas: It is important to develop continuing education for laity and clergy together!

2. Continuing education strictly for the clergy. Repeatedly, comments suggest that one or more of the seminaries be used strictly for this purpose. If such is done, many feel, "it will be most helpful if up-dating courses in *all* disciplines are included." "I feel most inadequate in what has happened in other disciplines since I was in college," says one minister. "I keep up fairly well in my own discipline by reading. But there is not time to read much in other disciplines. Some of my members who are able to watch TV a lot know more about what is happening than I do. There is seldom time for television."

Churches are not alone in the need for continuing education. Paul Armer, in his testimony before the U. S. Congress, pointed out recently that continuing education is a simple matter of necessity for all organizations: [6] "Individuals often become, over time, uneducated and therefore incompetent at a level at which they once performed quite adequately [he calls this the "Paul Principle"]. Part-time continuing education is going to be inadequate for many positions, and full-time continuing education is going to be more and more necessary." Mr. Armer advocated establishing full-time continuing education, somewhat like the social security system, because man must learn to adapt in a rapidly changing world, and society must provide mechanisms to help him.

3. Being and Doing

When responses first started arriving at the national Program Council office, a spot check of summaries indicated wide rejection of evangelism. Careful reading of the written comments, and just as careful listening at hearings, however, serves to correct that early misconception. What is rejected is a

[6] Paul Armer, Director of the Computation Center at Stanford, testified before the U. S. Congress on January 28, 1970. The testimony was published by the Committee on Science and Astronautics under the title "The Individual: His Privacy, Self-Image, and Obsolescence." For a copy of the report write the committee chairman, the Hon. George Miller, U. S. House of Representatives, Capitol Hill, Washington, D.C.

badly abused word. "Evangelism is no longer a word that communicates deep meaning," says one annual conference. Wide concurrence comes from across the country.

What respondents want to reflect about under this "church need" is commitment. More written comments were received on the subject of commitment than on any other subject, and in the summaries of over one hundred hearings, commitment emerges as essential. "Dealing with the meaning of commitment," say many groups, "is the key to dealing with all trends, with all issues, with all needs of the church." On the basis of *intensity* of comment and concern, commitment is seen as the highest priority of all. One bishop states: "Commitment is the most discussed subject at hearings that I have been conducting for several years. I can only conclude that United Methodists in my area believe with deep conviction that commitment is at the heart of all concerns."

United Methodists say they want to deal with commitment at two points: basic commitment to God through Jesus Christ and the commitment to one's fellowman that *must* result. "Without both facets," it is often asserted, "commitment becomes hollow and ingrown."

One reason many give for discarding the word evangelism is that too often the church's practice of it has been concerned only with commitment to God. Listen to one annual conference Committee on Evangelism: "We confess our sin of only enthusiastically 'evangelizing' with the first half of the Great Commandment. We have largely neglected 'and thou shalt love thy neighbor as thyself,' and only given lip service to it. It is our feeling that the church must now press for total commitment!"

"Such commitment must start with the fellowship itself. We have too often stopped with partial and shoddy commitment—sometimes no deeper than to the institution. No wonder, then, with institutionalism in question, many of our members have nothing left to which to be committed!" says another response.

"Let our members, first of all, ask 'What can I be?' Then, let them ask 'What can I do?' When they start out with the premise of being something, the doing naturally follows. The doing is then implemented with considerably less grumbling and foot-dragging. If you're committed to love, your love will make itself known in all sorts of ways that an unloving person can neither imagine nor program. If you are committed to compassion, you recognize opportunities to use it in ways that you would never have seen if you had simply gone out looking for something to 'do.' " So says a group from South Central, identifying themselves as evangelicals.

Written responses accompanying the tear sheets from *The Interpreter* indicate that more local church leaders feel that the church is doomed for neglect of basic, meaningful commitment to God, unless there is change, than for any other reason.

One such group of local church leaders echoes the feelings of many: "We have lost the ball game if we continue to take for granted that the church can have fruit without roots. By this we mean that there must be a more adequate communication (proclamation) of, and commitment to, the Christian faith (its meaning, its demands, its promises, its cost) that will make Christian fruits possible. The commitment must be supported (nurtured) by disciplines of study, meditation, worship, prayer (whatever words that might be used to describe 'new pieties') that are needed to keep roots deep in faith. Then, the fruits of social concern and Christlike love, too often missing, will flourish. The great sin in United Methodism is not apathy, nor is it unconcern. The great sin is shallowness." The lay chairman of the Administrative Board adds, "Changed men change society!"

An annual conference summary from North Central observes: "A rethinking of *commitment* is of most vital importance to The United Methodist Church. The tragedy of recent years has been that our challenge to commitment has been too shallow; it has been mostly to the institution. 'Join the church' has been the depth of our cry. Its very shallowness stands revealed now that institutionalism is in question. Persons whose commitment was only to the institution have little left.

98

Such people leave the church in droves—even such ministers. We must reevaluate that to whom we ask persons to make their commitment. Is not our commitment to Jesus Christ? Let's stop making it so easy to join the church! Let's stop judging success by the number on the roll! Let's clarify the meaning of commitment! If The United Methodist Church can clarify the meaning of commitment, and at the same time clarify the meaning of response in life because of that commitment, the other concerns of the church and of society will be properly dealt with!"

South Central conferences concur. One states: "Of the deepest concern to us is the failure of the church at present to *proclaim and live the gospel*—the unique feature of the church. Other organizations are better 'do-gooders' than the church and offer better social service. Of course the Christian life involves doing. But, first of all, it involves being. If we will clarify the meaning of being and the response of being, doing will be more nearly that which is the responsibility of the church. In recent years church leaders have been seemingly telling us that we pull ourselves up by our own bootstraps— that 'we' must do the job. What happened to our concept of being co-creators with God? What happened to seeking the source of our power and the guidance of God before doing anything? We strongly affirm the concerns of this document, but only if personal commitment and seeking for the leadership of God are given priority."

Another annual conference group emphasizes, "Commitment, commitment, commitment, commitment—no word received as much attention and concern in our annual conference. *This ought to be the Quadrennial Emphasis with the only offering that of people!*"

Many respondents write about a "fear of emotion" in The United Methodist Church. "We become more and more like the Church of England in John Wesley's day," observes a professor; "afraid of our emotions." Groups in South Central, Southeastern, Northeastern and Western Jurisdictions speak to the same subject. Look at their expressions in that order.

99

"Why are we afraid of a little emotion in our commitment? We aren't afraid to yell, cry, and laugh in the Cotton Bowl. Let's stop feeling that Christianity should be as quiet as a funeral parlor—actually quieter!"

"Why is our church afraid of giving a valid place to emotion in its 'intellectual' expression of faith? Emotion is considered to be valid in real life experiences."

"Enthusiasm and emotion should be included in our evangelism. That will stir up our respectable, cold, middle-class membership to the place that the fellowship will attract others. Wasn't it John Wesley who said that if you get people on fire for something, others will gather round to see what's burning?"

"Emotional appeals are still catching the imagination of men—witness television!"

4. I'm Ignoring You

United Methodists see the need for clear communication as vital for their church. In reacting to statements that communication channels need to be cleared, made two-way and speeded up, participants deal with many aspects of communication. The comments confirm a conviction that has been growing in the minds of denominational leaders; namely, that communicating to a constituency as varied as that of United Methodism, in the light of social upheaval, rapid change, and differing viewpoints, is a challenging but difficult task.

Some factors, say respondents, complicate communication between membership and leadership. "Many persons hear only what they want to hear—leaders as well as members." "Group caucuses are springing up in the annual conferences more interested in proclaiming their own position than in listening to others." "Grass-root leaders communicate to national leaders only that which they think national leaders want to hear. . . . National staff have a tendency to talk only to those at local levels who are already tuned their way." "We feel that denominational communicators are of the opinion that they must speak before all facts are in hand." "The present wave of anti-institutionalism creates a 'gulf of credibility' between bureaucrat and member that is difficult to bridge." "Our church members are more likely to believe what they read in a newspaper, or what some highly biased interpreter (like them) observes, than they are to believe what a communicator from headquarters sends out." "There are so many voices clamoring for attention today that persons are so numbed they have turned the raucousness to 'off.' "

Denominational communicators are aware of such problems and are working on them. Dr. Blaise Levai, who masterfully handles a part of the communication load for United Methodism's Board of Missions, observes that "the business of interpreting the religious scene in a revolutionary era is a tricky part of communication. Events such as James Forman's demand for reparations, and the Young Lords' take-over of a church, need reporters on religion who have a habit of looking closely at signs showing what people are crusading for and what changes they want. A sign bobbing amidst the usual 'Get Out of Vietnam *Now*' placards at a recent peace rally said simply, "Insufficient Data.' So much of religious reporting is an effort to gloss over insufficient data. When gaps appear, the communicator attempts to interpret the data, using past experiences as a guideline."

Dr. Levai also mulls over the fact that without response there is no communication: "An old riddle asks: Is there a sound in the forest if a tree crashes and no one is around to hear it? One thesis is that of Peter Drucker, who, in his recent essay 'Information, Communication and Understanding' (1970), says 'No.' There are sound waves, but there is no sound unless someone perceives it. Sound is created by perception.

"So the message of mission is powerless unless the church and its members are actively engaged in perceiving it, and are meaningfully in communication. Derived from the Latin, the word *communication* means an interchange of thoughts or ideas—a two-way exchange of views. When there is no response, communication is unlikely. . . . It may be that in all

101

the noise-making that besets our hearers, the messages are getting lost." [7]

Many focus their comments on the problem of communication being turned off because of disagreement with the message. Others say that the volume is turned way down not so much because of disagreement with the message but because there has not been wide involvement in formulating the viewpoint. For both reasons, receiving sets are off. This is reminiscent of a recent cartoon showing its main character with plugs in his ears. The caption reads, "I'm not hard of hearing! I'm ignoring you."

"Communication is very clear between church leaders and local churches," states the Council on Ministries of a huge local church in South Central. "The latter are just 'not buying,' to use a business indicator. In business this would tell us immediately that there is something needing attention in what we are trying to communicate. There is no communication without the receptivity of the hearer. Your potential hearers have turned off the 'commercial.' When there is something that they want to hear, they'll turn up the volume again. We don't suppose that the national church will hear this either—they won't want to."

A district Program Council summary from Southeastern concurs: "We don't find what you think or what you shout at us worth our time to listen. Maybe if we had been asked to express ourselves on the subject at hand, and maybe if we found that you listened to us, then maybe we might turn on our hearing aids."

"We have been hearing you all right," chimes in a lay group from North Central. "We don't like what we hear. And what we hear most clearly is that you have not been hearing one damn word we have been saying to you. But you will—when income gets bad enough."

An annual conference from the west adds: "What national

[7] Blaise Levai, "Mission as Communication: A Development Approach," unpublished essay. For further information contact Mr. Levai, United Methodist of Missions, 475 Riverside Drive, New York, N. Y. 10027

boards call a breakdown in communications is really what our conference members refer to as fundamental disagreement which board staff and bishops do not want to accept as reality.

"Another dimension did seem obvious in the replies from our conference, however, and it is this. 'The gatekeeper,' the switchboard operator, on what gets communicated is the local church pastor. Most admit that they only pass along what they think the traffic will bear. They say that they are sick and tired of communicating the flak that some isolated staff person sends out from his comfortable tower. Communication is cut off right there."

Thousands of comments center on the need for two-way communication. "The only way that you can clear up communications," says one lay group, "is to make it more than a one-way street." Many other groups and individuals echo this comment from the southeast: "The communication is clear, but who listens? Men in denominational seats of power seldom listen to ideas and opinions from local levels. You say that we don't hear you? When did *you* ever hear *us*?" Another group adds: "We hear that you believe that you are not communicating with us. What you call communication, we call *manipulation*. If it were communication, it would be two-way." Another says, "We've had enough of ivory-tower proclamations from Nashville and New York."

A pet peeve that comes in for a lot of attention by United Methodists is that of "jargon" in communications and writings. "Why don't church leaders put things into easily understood language?" asks one group. An annual conference in South Central, which used large numbers of instruments of their own design, asked for comments on communication. They summarize the feelings of their constituents as follows: "We have saturated people with words that don't get through. Consolidate the 'piles' (several definitions) of publications and *simplify* the language. Theologians and other church writers keep putting things in language to communicate in their own little circles. It *ain't* communicating with us or with the world! It is already true that you are just talking to yourselves. When are

103

you going to come down off your high horse and write things so that they communicate to other than experts? Our churches will not long continue to buy such stuff nor will they long continue to furnish you funds to publish it free!"

The feeling that church leaders are writing in their own professional jargon elicits a flood of comment. Many women's and laity groups reflect this attitude. So do clergy groups, like this one from North Central: "For too long the intellectuals of the church have been seemingly deathly afraid to publish anything in easily understandable language. Professionals seem to feel that their productions must be in the so-called professional jargon. Otherwise, they seem to feel, they may be looked down on by their peers. Also, church intellectuals seem to have fallen prey to intellectual faddism. We get the impression that they fear to let their position published today be the same as that published last year. (And they must publish—to maintain standing, to get promotions, and to receive raises in pay.) If their position remains the same, their peers may conclude they have stagnated, seems their phobia. Wonder why they don't communicate? We conclude that it is because they purposely obscure their thought in a professional jargon that is designed to communicate only with other professionals whose navel points are the same. They fail to communicate, too, we conclude, because they vacillate so swiftly from one theological position to another that no one places any confidence in their position of the latest moment."

Many United Methodists also feel that they are getting too many written communications, including newsletters and magazines. A North Central annual conference summary, with which the Program Council and its staff concur, says: "There are too many publications. *One* promotional journal should be enough! *Interpreter* fills that bill—put all effort into that. One good general church periodical should be enough! *Together* fills the bill—put all effort into that. All that other publications say to us is that 'up there' we have a bunch of egomaniacs who feel that the only way their great intelligence will get proper exposure is to have their own journal. The local church is fed up with this attempt to maintain position and power structure." An individual minister moans: "If I get any more communications across my desk—I'm dead! I would like fewer that say something." Many write that much of the money now committed to unwanted publications, "which is sinful," should be withdrawn and used for helping the poor. A large group of laity refer to the preoccupation of national boards with "their mountain of publications" as being the counterpart of the preoccupation of local churches with buildings.

Out of this wave of negative feeling, some creative suggestions in regard to communications have emerged. Respondents most often suggest that sincere attention be given to "two-way communication." A multitude of requests for more hearings, and more such samplings as this, were received.

The idea of establishing a "hot line" between national offices, area offices, and annual conference headquarters is strongly supported by the data. "We need immediate answers and immediate assistance very often—especially in interpreting and dealing with controversial issues." Some kind of hot line is seen as an answer. Dr. Bryan Brawner, Council on World Service and Finance, and Dr. Howard Greenwalt, Division of Interpretation, participated in a series of hearings throughout the denomination a year or so ago. At that time they heard requests for a hot line expressed with urgency, and interest is evidently growing. In this present sampling, expressions get more intense on this suggestion as data continue to come in.

Much interest is also expressed in making greater use of cassettes in all church programming. Respondents say that the necessary equipment is reasonably priced and readily available. "This is a dimension that appeals to our Program Council," states one annual conference. Many agree.

Others suggest exploring possible opportunities for denominational communication through educational cable TV systems. "Every educational institution in our state is tied together with private cable television," says one annual conference summary. "For the foreseeable future there will be a great number of unused channels available between these well-located centers. Our annual conference is doing a little experimentation in the use of the media for educational purposes. Groups assemble at the educational cable terminal centers and participate together around a central screen. Surely, there is potential here for the national church that merits investigation." The number of similar suggestions indicates that such cables are available, or soon will be, in many states.

So, it is seen, participating United Methodists are most loudly asking for two-way communication, for communication in which the kernel is cleared from the chaff of professional jargon, for resources developed with the participation of those whom they are designed to serve, and for the best use of new media.

5. Who Pays the Piper?

The second highest number of written comments on any subject were sent in on the subject of funding, yet there is the least agreement with the suggested statement of this need.

The field instrument statement on funding mentions the decline of financial giving through church channels; the fact that whereas contributors were formerly asked to give directly to certain needs and had personal contact with those needs, the contributor is now largely isolated from significant mission in his giving; and the fact that a "unified budget" with "qualified" leaders deciding where funds shall go is the best way to handle church funds.

Positions are stated forcefully and clearly, with many negative reactions to the statement that there is a decline in financial giving. "Not in our church," retorts an Administrative Board of a local church, "for our giving is the highest that it has ever been. It is true, however, that more is being spent locally and in the annual conference. Less is going through national church channels because of diminishing confidence in national leadership."

There is even more negative reaction to the statement that a unified budget expended by qualified persons is best. A cry for

106

opportunities to designate funds as a result of responsible personal involvement comes through loud and clear.

An interesting sidelight is the age-group response to the field instrument. The age group 45 through 54, who give very low priority to minority group demands, name more opportunities to designate funds as their number one priority.

And now, let's look directly at some of the most typical comments.

An annual conference group summary from South Central gives a concise scenario for funding that authentically speaks for a majority of participating United Methodists: "Five categoric areas of funding catch the attitudes of thousands in this annual conference:

"1. There are insistent demands for more chances to designate the program or project to which funds will go. Some see this as responsible involvement. Some see this as a way to control bureaucracy. Most all see this as a way to break out of the innocuous, unintelligible way United Methodists make apportionments. Clear signals are seen of the end to blind response to an asking.

"2. There is an obvious breakdown in confidence in unified budgets and in qualified leaders making the decisions as to expenditures of funds.

"3. Many threaten to use economic boycott in the church to get attention for how they feel. It is clearly the feeling that The United Methodist Church has made it clear that economic boycott is the way to register dissent and get attention.

"4. If the major thrust of the denomination is to fund social projects, as our people clearly believe, there are social projects in their own communities to which they feel more comfortable in committing their funds.

"5. Priorities for financial commitments must be reordered throughout the denomination. Our members feel that some things continue to get support just 'because we have always done so.' At least we should look to see if there is not a better way of funding some institutions, and if there are not some things we are supporting that no longer need support as urgently as other matters."

Stacks of requests for more opportunity to designate funds were received from all regions and from all groups. Among them are a large number of rather nostalgic, reluctant expressions from officers of United Methodism's Women's Society of Christian Service, a group traditionally committed to undesignated giving, that more and more persons are demanding opportunities to designate funds. Indicative of these is a comment from WSCS officers in the northeast. "People give," they observe, "when they know where, how, and by whom their money will be used. Their growing attitude in this regard is stimulated by their feeling that at present there is too much waste and duplication at every level of the church. They are asking, 'Whose idea is it that only national leaders are qualified to make decisions about use of funds?' Certainly that is not true if we are kept informed. More are feeling that it is a strange and egotistical claim to say that God's revelation and leading comes only to those in national positions of responsibility. A growing group express their feeling that leadership defends undesignated giving only to maintain the power which undesignated money gives to them. We have been proud that our women have given without benefit of designation. It begins to look as though designation will be more and more requested before funds are committed."

From others in the denomination come statements even more pointed. A Council on Ministries in a local church reflect the feeling of hundreds of other such groups when they say: "Unified budgets are efficient. Designated giving will get the money. We are now faced with a choice: efficiency with less funds or less efficiency with more opportunities to designate."

Great numbers of clearly stated, well-thought-out comments ask for opportunities to designate as a part of responsible involvement. A paragraph from an annual conference summary in North Central is typical:

"For many years church leaders have been urging, even demanding, that laymen arise from their apathy and find responsible involvement in the church and in society. A large number now stand ready to do so at all age levels. We interpret responsible involvement to mean committed, informed awareness which particpates in decision-making at all levels of the church *including the use of funds.* But now, we sense a reluctance on the part of the same church leaders to allow us the participation and responsible involvement that they have been challenging us to give. It is as though they believe that we would be irresponsible and make decisions based on old prejudices. Therefore, our leaders continue to make the decisions on the basis of their prejudices, old or new, however informed they may be. We are being awakened from apathy and noninvolvement. We are being awakened by preaching, by teaching, by confrontation, by polarization, by crisis-reaction. We will be involved in decision-making in The United Methodist Church. We will be involved in decisions as to how funds will be used—even if we must withhold them to get the chance. You have taught us that economic boycott can be used as a powerful tool to secure change and to get a chance for more involvement. We will use it in the church if we must."

A local church summary reflects: "Any program or project is worthy of a good salesman! Have you ordered your 1975 car yet? Do you think that you will just send the money to the company before you see it? We think not. You will feel better if you get to kick the tires, pound the hood, and slam the doors! We will feel better if you challenge us as to where a church of Jesus Christ should commit some funds, but let us make the decision."

From far and wide, however, respondents pick up the use of economic boycott as one reason for the growing demands for opportunities to designate contributions. Some want to control funds but see that approach as "no more evil than bureaucrats controlling funds." A comment from a local church Council on Ministries is typical: "Since The United Methodist Church by its actions (witness the Board of Missions action in connection with South Africa and sale of stock) has sanctioned the use of economic boycott for achieving its purposes and for calling attention to its prejudices as contrasted to other prejudices, you can expect a growing number of laymen and clergymen in the church to do the same. That is one great contributing factor to the growing tendency to withhold individual and group contributions from World Service[8] and to direct them toward matters considered to be more in line with what that individual or group believes. The national church is using the sanction. More and more individuals are doing so."

"What's good for the goose is good for the gander!" adds a district Program Council to a similar comment.

That there is a denominational breakdown in confidence in unified budgeting and in allowing "qualified" persons to decide the commitment of funds is clear from a wide variety of responses. A clergyman reflects, as do many: "I am a believer in the unified budget concept and have strongly supported it over the years. But the handwriting is on the wall. People will not support controversial causes with which they do not agree (or do not understand enough to know whether they agree). Controversial causes must be set by themselves in seeking support, or all causes will suffer—they already have. If we believe in new concepts of freedom, I suppose, we must grant to the individual the full rights of self-determination—including where his money goes."

A group summary from the northeast picks up the refrain: "Unified budget? No! Persons are now willing to give only to definite causes, thus knowing where and how their money will be used and thus seeing tangible results in line with *their* understanding of Christian commitment. Those persons are no longer interested in the commitments of 'qualified' bureaucrats. Many of us worked with some of those when they were in the annual conference. We know their foibles along with their qualifications. Some of them have just found a wider arena and more money to use in *paternalistic* service."

[8] World Service in United Methodism is an annual apportionment to each local church for support of denominational agencies as well as national and world mission.

The comments continue to come. An overwhelming number jump on the idea of "qualified" persons deciding "how our money shall be spent." Whatever the reasons may be, anti-institutional, anti-bureaucratic, or anti-whatchamacallit, there is a crisis in confidence. "The 'qualified' to whom you refer seem to have little wisdom and less judgment," says an annual conference summary from Southeastern. And a conference lay leader from North Central growls: "I feel that giving each of my kids a Cadillac so that they can pick up other kids for the youth fellowship meeting is as relevant for a Christian as many of the expenditures that are being made by church leaders, . . . more so than the fantastic amounts we spend for parsonages for our district superintendents and the Program Council staff."

But, change the scene. Many are the comments reflecting that the denomination acts more and more like "just another social agency." "If so," says an annual conference Program Council, "we see no reason why we should not commit our funds to the urgent social issues of our own area."

A group from a large urban church in the northeast go into their feelings more deeply: "When the church tries to duplicate the work of social agencies (and poorly so because of committee confusion and ignorance), the money from our members begins to go more to social agencies, locally based, with which members are personally acquainted and which follow policies in which members believe. In other words, when the church tries to be just another social agency, it does so poorly, and asks for support of our members to be redirected to local agencies that do a better job. Incidentally, local agencies will happily share an itemized budget with their members and contributors. The boards of The United Methodist Church will not—even when asked! Why? Why? Why?"

One other facet of funding that receives much interest is "the need for the church to reorder her priorities." From all regions comes the request for national guidance in studying the long-range support of church-related institutions. "The church needs to examine her continuing support of any in-

111

stitution. Is there still the need for the church to be in the 'institutional' business that there was at the time such institutions were started? Can the church realistically support institutions over the years and still have resources to commit to urgent missional concerns? Would some institutions be better supported by local, state and national government at this point in history? How much of the funds that the church commits to institutions actually help those most deeply in need? Honestly, in looking at our own, we have to say, 'Not much!' These and other questions need to be asked everywhere in the church now," observes one annual conference Program Council in South Central.

An annual conference group in Southeastern reflect even greater urgency—almost consternation—when they state: "Our annual conference is so burdened with the support of six church-related colleges that there is no chance of real commitment of funds to needed local mission. Worse is the fact that the amount we give to these colleges will not be enough to save some of them. They will not weather the financial storm they are in unless greater financial assistance can be found than the church is able to give. The day of reckoning is at hand. The church cannot continue to support these colleges over the long haul and meet its other missional obligations as well." They, too, are asking for a look at what long-range financial priorities should be.

A large number of participants want the Council on World Service and Finance to investigate more productive ways of handling investment portfolios for the denomination. Many who offer the suggestion define productive not as "making the most money" but as "committing investments to missional concerns in line with Christian purpose while drawing some income as well." They speak of the huge investment portfolios of some general agencies, the significantly large pension investments owned by annual conferences, and the possibility of a general investment fund in which interested individuals could place contributions "the income of which can assist in financing mission of the church." "At least, the General Conference should examine the possibilities," say numbers of individuals and groups in United Methodism.

Comments on funding have grown continuously in number and in intensity. Feelings expressed have made necessary the retitling of this church need from "cultivation for funds" to "requests for more opportunities to designate funds." Indications are that by the time this book is published, the growing crescendo of response on the subject of funding will have moved this church need higher in the priority listing.

8

NEEDS: SPRING CLEANING

> The church follows her Lord with a troubled soul and anxious heart—tempted again and again to give up the whole issue of mission and seek shelter in conformity to the status quo, becoming house servant of the times. But such conformity will not do, for the church knows, as her Master knew, that she is here not to save herself but the world, and that for this cause she has come to such an hour. —Bishop W. Ralph Ward

With as much intensity of feeling, but indicating less priority, United Methodists reflect on four other church needs. From the comments submitted, we shall again look at those most typical of people's feelings.

6. The Uncertain Trumpet?

The field instrument invites reaction to the statement that theology and values stand in need of clarification and understanding. The church is uneasy in what it says about beliefs and values, and an "affirmational theology" must be developed in language understandable to secular man.

The response is quite mixed. Requests for resources on theology and values are more than 25 percent higher than requests in any other category of church needs. The age group 45 through 54 come into the picture again, indicating theology and values as their third priority. "Our muddy thinking in values and theology is what has the church in the mess it is in," says an attorney in that age span. From communities of less than five hundred persons come expressions of even higher priority. Young adults and youth express less priority; their comments indicate that they are more "functional" and less "creedal" in their outlook: "Our certainties will emerge from getting with it and not from talking about it."

"We have an affirmational theology now," sums up a conference group in the southeast. "We are just afraid to affirm it. We are becoming pessimistic, afraid that God is dead, expressing defeat and frustration. Our timidity appeals to no one! Our need is that of reclaiming certainty. God is alive and equal to the contemporary." So reflect the majority.

There are clear signs, however, in much of the written comment, of a desire for clarification of theology. Methodists are calling for theology that is "based on knowledge of God rather than assumptions about the world"; that is "optimistic, radiant, and courageous"; and that is "developed as laity and clergy consider theology together."

Respondents set forth their conviction that "the present uncertainty in theology is due to the confusion and uncertainty expressed by church leadership." "No wonder members are lukewarm, disgusted, and lacking in commitment," says an annual conference in the southeast. "Our leaders are! In the literature coming from national boards and from seminaries the impression is generated that there is utter chaos about what the church should believe and do." "Who will gather if the trumpet give an uncertain sound?" chimes in a South Central conference. "Of course, we need certainty! But keep professional jargon out of it. A seminary professor addressing our conference this year said, in quoting Moltmann, 'I think I understand what Moltmann means by this. I need to talk to him to be sure.' If a theologian is not certain about meanings in theological writing, how can we be?"

The disenchantment between church and seminary comes out strongly again in relation to theology. One who participated in the first summary discussions of these data remarked: "It would seem that respondents commented more on their antagonism for seminary professors than they did on theology."

115

Typical of that response is a comment from the summary of feelings in an annual conference in North Central: "If by development of theology you mean by seminary professors, the answer is no! They have spoken in derision of the church and what it believes for long enough. With only a few exceptions, they are engaged in running dialogue only with each other—certainly not with the church and churchmen. The seminaries have no sympathy for the local church and little for the denomination. 'Let the blind lead the blind' has no appeal for our members. Clarification of theology will come from the firing line and not from the professionals."

Faddism in theology generates much negative reaction, as we have already seen. "What is the theological fad of the morning?" asks a group from a local church. "We haven't yet seen the latest dispatch from headquarters."

Members from local areas are not alone, however, in questioning the quick acceptance of theological fads. Dr. Paul Minear of Yale University Divinity School says: "Our theological reflections, stimulated by crises as they are, are often based on fads and assume more permanence than they have. Classical theology of the church will prove more lasting than the miniskirted theology of our day."

When we leave these more negative comments on theological development, the more positive see theology as a "continuing process of conversation and reflection between the tradition and hope within which we stand and the history in which we participate." Theology then is not seen so much a scholastic discipline as it is an "emergence from full participation, reflection, and dialogue."

The Women's Society officers in an annual conference in the northeast contribute their thinking on theological symbols and theological resymbolization. "If present theological symbols have lost their meaning, we in the church (who have been using them) are to blame. We leave meaning out of our usage of them, and then make them ambiguous by our hypocritical living. We need to put consistent meaning into whatever symbols we use! Just gathering new symbols will be meaningless unless we gather new meaning. It is our feeling that if Christian disciples make their living consistent with the symbols they use, those symbols will be alive—whether old or new. Live symbols communicate!"

Clearly, United Methodists are deeply concerned about rethinking "the values on which decisions are made." Participants are aware that accepted value systems are under close scrutiny. One group sees the uncertainty about value systems reflected in "the rapid suggestion in our time of legalistic ethics, situation ethics, contextual ethics, anticipatory ethics, and large general principles as bases for decisions."

Most participants seem to feel that the church must give immediate attention to values and morals. The scientist cries for assistance in basic decisions about the use of his science. The physician cries for clarification of values in regard to organ transplants. The ordinary person in a secular society questions the value of the practical decisions he must make each day. "What does the church have to say?" ask most who respond.

Large numbers of comments ask the church to develop models for ethical decision-making in all contexts of modern culture. They want leadership from the church, but they do not feel they are getting it at present. A United Methodist scientist working in a major industrial corporation says, "I have looked to the church for leadership and guidance in ethical decision-making, but frankly I have found more help from my own colleagues." The call is strong for the church to give leadership to such a man and his colleagues in developing a model for ethical decisions in the context of their work. We have already heard a similar plea from physicians.

One thing is clear. The vast majority of respondents are seeing the need for all persons to find ethical and human ways of using "their power." The consensus backs Sir Theodore Fox, who says in *Lancet*, "We shall have to learn to refrain from doing some things merely because we know how to do them."

Obviously, too, no one in this sample favors "firm positions and denominational pronouncements." "No glass slipper fits every princess," says a local church group. "Individuals must be nurtured in the church to make their own decisions. We must then rely upon those individuals to make the best decisions possible," adds a group of youth.

Harvey Cox, in *On Leaving It to the Snake*, stimulates our thought on changing values. "We live in a world which can never again look an absolute moral principle in the face without asking for its ideological credentials. In this world of competing relativisms, what can the Church do? Should it cling with increasing ferocity to its cherished 'principles,' many of them spawned in a robust period of frontier individualism, and decry 'moral collapse' around it? This has been the posture of the dying remnant of every ancient regime in history. Or should it realize that the Christian gospel is *not* the summons to a particular moral code at all—but a living enactment, the coming kingdom initiated by Jesus? The gospel is a word addressed to moral cynics and ethical absolutists alike, a word which finds all our ethical pretensions filthy rags and reconciles men to each other with no reference to their level of moral attainment."

7. Breaking the Mold

In responding on this church need, United Methodists are reacting to a statement that "varying forms of ministry for widely differing situations will need to be developed in the church in contrast to ministry singularizing around a local parish form as at present."

General agreement with the statement is low. The most agreement is registered in the largest communities and in the largest churches. Single persons give their number one priority to developing new forms of ministry, youth give it high priority, but the age group 45 through 54 give it the least priority of any. Most respondents strongly support a broad-based ecumenical approach for developing new ministries, if such is to be done.

118

Participants seem to assume that the paragraph in the field instrument implies doing away with the local parish. Quick and vigorous is the defense of the parish, "even though its form and practice may need change."

The local parish is the reasonable "base" for new ministries, many feel. From a North Central annual conference summary comes a typical opinion: "It seems to us that the power base of the local parish must be behind new forms of ministry in order to supply personnel, needed finance, and, especially, continuity. Most new ministries tried in our conference without that base lasted only as long as the tenure of the person who organized them. Without a financial base that leader spent most of his time getting a few dollars with which to operate. When that leader was moved, in typical church style, the new ministry disintegrated. On the other hand, the new ministries sponsored by, and undergirded by, a local church (too few, we admit) have kept going and have had needed resources."

Appreciation for a team ministry concept is voiced widely by those who participated. An annual conference in the northeast observes: "More team ministries are needed. But the *status* of such ministries needs to be up-graded in the thinking of both laity and clergy—and especially in the thinking of the cabinet. It should not be considered a demotion for a minister to go to such a team from a station appointment—but it is! Team ministries are needed in both rural and urban areas; they make a lot of sense. Expertise of many kinds can be brought onto such a team. One group of persons in our conference makes the following observation: 'Why should ten ministers in our county spend as much time in sermon preparation as they do when all of them together preach to less than 1,500 persons on an average Sunday? Why not one good preacher on a team with ministers of other expertise? With the combined salaries paid in those ten churches, we should be able to build a team of fewer bodies who could serve all churches and persons better because of training and experience.' " Team ministry possibilities are mentioned positively

119

many times. Both denominational and ecumenical teams are suggested.

Most response strongly favoring new forms of ministry originates with youth and young adults. A university student group in North Central suggests: "The United Methodist Church had better be trying some new forms of ministry! The old forms are no longer getting much response. Anyway, why does worship have to be in the same old form in the same old way at the same old time? Maybe it's more important that we sleep on Sunday morning, you know, rest! Maybe it's more meaningful to use music that we know and forms that grab *us*—not those that grabbed Methusaleh. Why not? Why not study in new forms, at new times, and maybe not even in an expensive building? Why not Monday school classes?"

A relatively new congregation, mostly young adults, takes up the cry: "Our discussion group came up with having the sermon at the first worship hour, small discussion groups on the sermon subject the second hour (sometimes with other resources), followed by suggested task forces on a volunteer basis for needed follow-through. The congregation and our pastor are excited about the whole idea. This questionnaire stimulated the whole idea. Thanks!"

A North Central urban ministers' association, however, expresses many people's apprehension that the denomination will probably try to "overorganize new ministries as it has almost everything else. Just let new ministries happen," they plead, "and approve of them when they do. . . . Don't try designing them complete with guidebook, stilted literature, and, oh yes, the offering." A substantial number of such comments came in.

8. Simplify, Simplify, Simplify

Youth, males, and clergy find greater reason to look for more workable church organizational forms than do others. But although United Methodists as a whole give this church need a low priority, they apparently do so because they believe in the present church organization. "We need adjustments, not radical changes," many participants say. They definitely express strong feelings for making adjustments, however.

Some fear that tinkering with the machinery may be just an excuse to avoid coming to grips with more important matters. "Let the church face up to needed function, much of which is noted in questions in this instrument, and let needed forms develop and unneeded forms die."

Bishop James Armstrong reminds his readers that there are more important needs facing the church than debating forms. In his incisive book, *The Urgent Now,* he says: "While we are debating the legitimacy of the new forms and liturgies in our churches, a mushroom cloud gathers on the far horizon and everything we hold dear teeters at the abyss of a new Dark Age." His thought is supported by many.

Several annual conference groups reflect that they got the cart before the horse in the restructuring of their own operating structure. "Without asking what function was needed, we restructured. Now, we know that all we did was reshuffle and that we are continuing business as usual. Don't do that at the national level. In many ways such a reshuffling does not work as well as the old ways. We ended up with more expense, with more 'needed' meetings, and with less persons involved in the decision-making." That South Central comment is heartily seconded by a North Central conference: "Our leadership has simply reshuffled the old deck, realigned and renamed old structures, loudly proclaimed 'new structures for new mission,' and ended up doing the same old thing."

A large majority of United Methodists see a need for "streamling and cutting dead timber from the organization." "Simplify, simplify, simplify, simplify" were the only words in the summary from an annual conference in the west. Strong expression favors giving up outmoded forms when they no longer serve people, and trying new models within the present organization.

Mel Blake, former Methodist missionary and Board of Missions executive, observed recently that there are many forms that continue within the organization, the reason for which is long forgotten. "It reminds me," he says, "of a husband watching his wife prepare a ham for baking in the oven. As he watched, she cut off one end of the ham square, turned the ham and cut off the other end square, and put the ham into the oven to bake. 'Why did you cut that ham like that?' asked her husband. 'Because my mother always did,' the wife replied. So, the curious husband asked his mother-in-law the same question. 'Grandma always did it,' was the answer. Grandma was then asked for an explanation. 'Sakes alive, honey,' replied Grandma, 'my baking pan was too short!' " Many comments indicate a feeling that there is little more reason for continuing some practices in present church organization. New forms may better fit present situations.

The data plead for openness to innovative, flexible organizational forms, perhaps temporary, and for willingness to allocate all types of resources to such new models. Many feel that from such new experience more workable organization can and should evolve.

In commenting on the need for new forms of organization, Warren Bennis observes: "What we need desperately is not department stores but boutiques, . . . smaller units with sharply focused distinctive competence. . . . Somebody has to build alternative models, keep the pressure on, invent new living-learning communities. Without this yeasty element nothing can happen in existing organizations." Hundreds of comments express eagerness to try this approach in the denomination.

United Methodists express a growing recognition that there is no longer any such thing as only one way of operating. Neither is there "such a thing as only one congregation in the local church. There are many congregations!" "The pluralism of society, and a myriad of life styles, is *in* as well as out of the church. Many of our members have stopped worshiping and studying not because they have lost interest in Christianity but because worship and study are only slanted to one life style and to one viewpoint. So, these persons start house chapels, underground churches, etc. Too many of our churches take the attitude, 'If they don't like the way we do things, why don't they go somewhere else?' That narrow, bigoted approach drives many sincere persons away. Why do we not plan worship and study of many forms for the many life styles within a single congregation? Continue old forms as long as they appeal to any. Try new forms for those who want them. Learn from each other. The church should be big enough for differing opinions and for differing approaches." So a Western conference summary states a position. Many agree. Many comments tell of new life being breathed into old congregations by offering concurrently traditional and contemporary worship patterns, Sunday school classes and seminar elective classes, old organizations and new task forces.

We have already heard the clamor for more lay participation in United Methodism. Thousands of persons add comments about that subject in connection with reflection on "workable organization."

Many ask for decentralization within the organization of a special kind: the "decentralization of national board staff whose purpose is to serve the annual conferences, districts, and local churches." Such comments reason that staff located regionally will be closer to the local church and more aware of its needs, more readily available to annual conferences when they need consultative assistance, and better able to be a communication link between national board and the local church. A large number of comments speak of reluctance to ask for national staff help from "distant headquarters cities." "We do not always know what help we need. We just know that we need help. Yet our conscience bothers us to ask someone to come great distances just to 'rap' with us. Get service staff closer to us." So says an annual conference hundreds of miles from any headquarters city. Such conferences speak with great appreciation for the few general board service staff located presently at local levels.

Closely related to decentralization of staff is an even more urgent request to have leadership training closer to the place where leadership must be exercised. A South Central annual conference program staff catches the feelings of most when they say: "Too often our national agencies have taken a few persons out of the local church and have taken them 'away' to a camp or a center for training. Nothing much resulted! Upon their return home they were either unable to apply or communicate what you intended for them to learn, or they were afraid to do so because the attempt might meet with resistance. We need training closer to the local church, . . . not workshops in a 'foreign' setting where the environment often bears little resemblance to that in which our leaders operate back home. Lab training, for instance, for our under-equipped, poorly motivated teachers in an 'ideal setting' only raises the frustration level of our leaders. We need training teams who can work in the setting where leadership takes place. Use camps and centers to train the trainers. Send the trainers into the settings where battles are fought."

Before leaving the matter of leadership training, we should look at the large number of comments that while the district superintendency in United Methodism is the genius of the denomination's system, people assigned to this supervisory office are often not trained for it. Many feel that district superintendents should have special training in management. They are seen as managers in the best sense of the word, and it is especially necessary for them to be trained in the human elements of managing. Then they should be freed from detail work that keeps them from functioning in the most helpful way.

Next, the matter of "meetings, meetings, meetings" comes in for much attention. Ministers blame meetings for not allowing them to do a better job. One minister spoke out at a recent Chicago meeting and said: "I worked my head off for a week to get my parish in order so I could come to this meeting. I'll work my head off for a week when I get home just to get caught up. In other words, everything I do is crisis. I don't have time to design creative program. When I get caught up, I'll start getting ready for my next meeting."

Laity seem to sense this feeling on the part of ministers. The laity blame "required" meetings for the fact that ministers are "gone all of the time." "Our minister is required to be at so many meetings that all he has time to do at home is prepare his sermons. Why so many meetings?" Other lay persons reflect that ministers love to be away at meetings to avoid facing demanding work at home.

Laity also wonder about their own involvement in meetings. One layman, who identifies himself as a member of the Board of Education of the denomination, says: "I find myself expending all of my energy and talent attending conferences, consultations, workshops, seminars, happenings, etc. I am called to the national, jurisdictional, area, and conference levels for meetings. Most of what little time I have remaining is spent in filling out forms for some general agency. This morning I met my pastor on the street. He asked me when I was going to start giving some time to my local church. I replied, 'Now!' I will not continue to waste my time and my church's money in such busy tommyrot. Bishop Kennedy was right—God deliver us from meetings."

Still, meetings go on and people flock to attend. United Methodism's General Conference became concerned enough to adopt a resolution asking that national meetings be coordinated. The idea was to reduce the number of such meetings needed. Instead, meetings seem to be proliferating. Some groups form unofficial organizations to arrange for national meetings, with sponsorship and financial support from official agencies, and claim that their meetings do not come under the scope of the resolution. "Meetings shall probably continue to go on until no one shows up," remarks a group of district superintendents. That could happen. One bishop reports that he is considering asking his annual conferences to take action instructing their members to stay at home. Lay attitudes indicate that such a motion would find quick support.

Last but not least in the area of organizational forms is the flood of expression from United Methodists pleading for more realistic planning at all levels of the denomination. Mirroring most of these is an observation from an annual conference summary in the southeast: "Badly needed are consultants in

125

planning. Guidelines and articles do not get the job done. A 'live' consultant, trained in group process, helps to get planning on the track; print does not. We feel that consultants who are knowledgeable about planning approaches, who are not trying to 'sell' one way of doing the job, who are patient enough to lead a group in thinking through what their own planning approach should be, and who, at the same time, are committed to the church will help to get more vital relevancy into the church than all the resolutions of all the boards put together. . . . The church has been good at seeing issues, anticipating change, and gathering data. The church is wanting in examining data through the eyes of purpose, in understanding what it takes to get follow-through, and in evaluation. We are wanting in those matters at every organizational level. From our conference study, we conclude that a lot of noise is being made throughout the church about mission, but that we are getting too little done. Genuine planning will be a real help, our leaders feel." Another annual conference in the northeast closes a similar statement with the words, "And with training in planning we need training in problem-solving, conflict management, and understanding pluralism. We have antagonism and resistance with all three."

Along with the plea for assistance in planning is the urgent request to "keep the information flow going both ways." A South Central annual conference summary bubbles: "The laymen of our annual conference have expressed genuine enthusiasm for the opportunity to express themselves 'right to the top.' We are getting repeated expressions such as, 'This is the first time there has been any indication that national leaders care what we think,' and, 'At last someone has realized that we too may have some intelligence and awareness.' You will note in the sample comments which we are sending to you with our summary that there is a large incidence of appreciation at being asked to participate in this sample. We are finding similar enthusiasm expressed for the hearings we are holding in local churches. One local church wrote in, 'It was great! The hearing helped to restore confidence in the conference staff. Our members have been wondering why we even need you fellows. Now our people are chattering about the fact that someone came to listen to us. Do it again—and soon.' Such enthusiasm reinforces the genuineness of the commitment of laity to want to participate. They seem to want sincerely to hear and be heard. We hope that the Program Council keeps this process going. Count us in!"

9. Connectionalism: A Paper Tiger?

In reflecting on United Methodism's traditional connectional system, participants express substantial support for it. Because of that support, they tend to give the matter low priority, as we have seen in chapter 2. The field instrument did, however, stimulate a number of comments on specific dimensions of connectionalism.

Some connections are felt to be missing. From every annual conference group comes agreement with this comment from North Central: "The only thing wrong with our connectional system is that some of the connections are missing—rather, ignored! Leadership at national and conference levels have been acting as though they are *the* connection—not just one important part of it. Give the local church a chance to be connected rather than dominated and manipulated. One thing will help. Limit tenure in all board and administrative jobs to twelve years—then back to the local church to work! Our churches are saying that leaders speak with so little appreciation of the local church that they must 'really be out of it!' "

A conference summary from Northeastern says: "We are kidding ourselves by thinking that our connectionalism in properly working at the present time. To a large degree, it is a great idea but a 'paper tiger.' Some of our churches, so big that they throw their weight around or so small that no one cares what they do, operate like congregational churches. The average church, on the other hand, is held under the thumb of the hierarchy. We are profaning such operation by calling it connectional. We believe in a connectional system that allows

127

the average minister, the average lay person, the average local church, the average staff person, to function in a connected way!"

The missing connection of "upfeed" is played upon by an annual conference group in Southeastern: "There is nothing really wrong with our organization if we allow it to work the way it was designed. Clean it up, coordinate activities, do away with volumes of worthless materials, simplify the national structure, and eliminate most of the promotional meetings. . . . Have upfeed before downfeed! If that happens, we shall welcome stimulation by our leaders. The problem now is that we have all 'stimulation' with no listening. Local churches will not be pushed around by executives . . . any longer. If they are recognized as participants in the connection, if they are listened to, they will be willing to listen." A loud chorus sings much the same melody. "Connectionalism is supposed to be a partnership"; "the greatest threat to connectionalism is that of national boards assuming false sovereignty"; "if connectionalism degenerates into bureaucratic manipulation, it will swiftly die" —so the chorus swells.

Others say decentralization is a must. We have already listened to requests for decentralization of national staff who serve the local areas and for bringing all leadership training closer to "the arena where the game is played," the local church. Other indicative expressions on decentralization speak of the problem of decision-making.

As other institutions of society are hearing, so The United Methodist Church is called upon to hear in these data a cry to "get decision-making back closer to the local church." "Priorities must be determined *with* the participation of the local church if there is to be implementation! More local autonomy must be allowed (trust) about *how* priorities are to be dealt with—how the job is to be done. Prod local churches all you want to as long as it is *with* their participation, and as long as it is recognized that the final decision on strategy is theirs. Don't hand us any more packaged programs! No matter how good they may be, such manipulation turns us off," says the summary from a group of local churches working in coalition.

Out of the hundreds of summaries submitted by local churches, it is the exception to find one that does not contain such a statement. The plea is not for more decentralization of national agencies, except for staff who serve local areas, but for more decentralization of the decision-making. An executive of a Detroit automobile corporation believes this feeling is valid. He says, "General Motors will never make the mistake of offering only one model to its constituency with the implied attitude, 'Buy it or walk.' For the same reasons, the Methodist corporation needs to offer more options."

Another cry in these data is for more coordination and simplification in organizational operation. An indicative comment from a denominational executive states that in the United Methodist connectional system "general and conference agencies are seen as a professionally controlled, cumbersome, inefficient superstructure that serves the local church less and less. Most people to whom I talk want to close offices, clean house, and put more resources behind mission in local areas. Either the battle will be won at local levels, they feel, or it will be lost. I am hearing members say that such questions as the following should be asked. Are we writing curriculum materials that someone else is already doing better? Are we not just spinning our wheels by writing pronouncements on social issues that never get implemented? Would it not be better to reach connectional decisions by a process that would involve local areas in developing a position for the whole of the connection? Does the overhead expense of United Methodist operation stand scrutiny in the light of supporting the best Christian service to *people*? Maybe the answers are yes, maybe no, but we had better be looking with honesty and a willingness to 'tune up' the connections when change seems warranted. Members are forming their own answers based on meager information, because national agencies will not provide better information."

Picking up on the need for coordination, a Western annual

conference group says: "There is a growing demand for genuine coordination at all levels in the denomination—national, jurisdictional, and annual conference. Duplication and overlapping are being seriously questioned in a time when local churches are finding it more and more difficult to finance 'their own thing.' 'Why should we continue to contribute to the production of unwanted and unusable material when we have been forced to discontinue our own newsletter?' they ask. 'We see no reason to send money that backs innocuous national meetings when we have had to cut from our budget for next year the money to send our youth to summer church camp,' they say. Greater care is needed in what is printed and in what meetings are held. Certainly leadership training enterprises can be placed together in leadership schools. Certainly the General Conference or someone can crack down on the competition for power evident in the operation of national boards. They cry about not knowing how to communicate with the annual conference when what they really have in mind is that their own little power structure has been eliminated in the annual conference. They know how to communicate with us all right! They must do so through the Program Council, but they don't want to. The national boards are just not showing a willingness to take their chances in the total arena of needed program. They want back their little conference board that they can better manipulate. We like, on the other hand, coordinated programming approach with every concern standing on its own bottom without undue pressure from *up there*. Unless the bureaucracy is willing to move in the direction of allowing more flexibility at local levels, national staff will find themselves a locomotive chugging up a siding with no cars following, local conferences will be taking the cars up a different track." (I have read so many references to the symbol of a locomotive chugging up the track with no cars following that I find myself waking up with nightmares of angry locomotives about to devour me.)

Another facet of connectionalism which respondents believe needs polishing is that of clear communication within the system. This has already been discussed, but it must be repeated here. "No one in the local church 'hears' what happens at General Conference, at annual conference, at district conferences, or at a national meeting. Whatever channels you have been depending upon don't work."

9

SOME DEAD HORSES AND
A FEW COLTS ABORNING

> "Your plane is not in from Seattle yet, sir," she said. "There will be a slight delay."
>
> "I happen to have information on that flight," I said. "The plane is actually at this moment still circling Moose Jaw while the pilots study a 1938 Texaco road map. They've been lost for an hour and are running dangerously low on sugar coated gum tablets and little dry sandwiches."
>
> "But in a larger sense," said Nancy, "aren't we all still circling Moose Jaw?"
>
> —Richard Bissell, *Still Circling Moose Jaw*

One day I was discussing with Alan Waltz, who heads United Methodism's Research Section, the attitudes submitted by participants in this sample. As we scanned the most indicative expressions, it became apparent that there were some subjects in which the majority voiced little, if any, interest—unless it was antagonism. Four subject areas stood out in particular, and Dr. Waltz remarked, "You may have to write a chapter on the Four Dead Horses of the Christian Apocalypse!" Since the Apocalypse, like these data, points toward the future, this does seem to be an obligation.

Continuing consideration of the data also reveals another side—some possible "colts aborning." There are feeling areas where expression about what is needed is so intense that we dare not neglect them. Some fresh mounts seem to be waiting in the corral to be saddled and ridden.

The topics of this chapter are especially interesting because of their spontaneity. For the most part, the comments are unpremeditated and impulsive—at least there is little in the field instrument to directly stimulate the number and intensity of them. The fact that most appear at the end of the field instrument seems to indicate that people could not bring themselves to send it in until they had gotten something "off their chest," as one put it. Often the comments are marked with a big asterisk or a huge check mark. Look at this, the respondents seem to be saying; there is something here that is important!

Some Dead Horses?

First, let's look at some aspects of church life to which Methodists gave low priority, even though spontaneous comments were numerous and lengthy. Four areas come under this heading: any further national organic church union, denominational pronouncements, outworn ecclesiastical vocabulary, and bureaucratic manipulation. Comments from all over the church tend to agree on some glaring faults—dead horses, for sure.

Ecumenicity, Yes! Merger, No!

The very thought of any further national organic church union draws intensely negative blasts. Only a few respondents, mostly women, seem to favor COCU, abbreviation for a proposed merger plan of major Protestant denominations presently under consideration in the Consultation on Church Union. Even from the women, negative expressions outweigh the positive.

Youth comments see any further national organic church union as bringing into being "a bigger and bigger of that which is needed less and less," by which they apparently mean bureaucracy. "Quit wasting what remains of church influence," injects a university group from South Central, "on building a bigger mousetrap. We are not as concerned with the petty divisions in the church as we are with the church's damning uninvolvement with burning issues! Let's get with it!" A high school group from United Methodism's Youth Fellowship

133

adds, "If Rome is not involved in proposed merger, forget it! We want no Protestant Vatican."

Early in the process of data gathering, a tear sheet was printed in United Methodism's national program journal, *The Interpreter,* which specifically included ecumenicity. The question asked if an evaluation of ecumenical involvement was necessary in the light of proposed organic church union and possible loose, working coalitions of denominations to get a job done. The answer was a resounding "no" to further organic church union and a resounding "yes" to coalitional working relationships. At that time more written comments were submitted on ecumenicity than on any other topic.

When the more widely used field instrument was designed, leaders from local areas encouraged us to decide not to include the subject of organic church union. We waited with curiosity to see if there would be spontaneous comments on the subject. To use an expression my grandfather coined, we were "flabberteegasted" by the write-ins. The largest number of spontaneous comments came in on this subject, and they consistently agree with the viewpoint expressed by respondents to the earlier tear sheet and with hearing summaries from across the country. But we should let some of the comments speak for themselves.

A group summary from a North Central annual conference speaks for many: "In general, our members express little interest in ecumenical church union. Expressions are heavily more antagonistic than favorable to any further unions. Our membership feels that the mergers which have been consummated were so expensive, so time-consuming, so involved in selfish fears and accommodations that their negative aspects have more than offset their advantages. Many feel that we have succeeded in bringing into being a more cumbersome institutionalism. We have an overwhelming feeling that merger involvements have set our conference back in mission from five to ten years. Assumed debts alone drain off funds that might otherwise have been used for local mission."

"Expressions in the field of ecumenicity are quite appreciative, however," admits another summary from an annual conference in the northeast, "of loosely organized, coalitional, functional ecumenical relationships to get wider involvement in urgent mission. Such working together strengthens both the participant and the mission. Our people want to find where denominations can work together and get about it. In that way any denomination can participate when such participation is seen as valid in their own decision-making A denomination can also stay out without stigma attached. If merger is needed, let it come out of functioning together."

These two comments are indicative of what most are saying. The general feeling is stated succinctly by a group of ministers in New York City who say simply, "Functional ecumenicity, yes! Organic merger, no!" Several hearing groups of ecumenical workers concur.

Numerous group comments referred with appreciation to the views on church union of Bishop Gerald F. Kennedy in *While I Am on My Feet*: "Now the proponents of church union argue that it could be loose in its polity and everybody could be just as free as they are now. But if this were actually the case, there would be little sense in changing what we have. It would be better to strengthen our councils and perfect our means of cooperation. Every real union means that we all give up something. But if there are strong differences of opinion as to what is essential in the faith, I can hardly ask my fellow Christian to surrender his essential but allow me to keep mine. I would rather say that we shall both keep our essentials and work together in the faith which we hold in common."

Another dimension of possible ecumenical relationship brought out by a lively minority is that of renewed conciliar movement. Although the expression is from a smaller group, it is avid enough to deserve mention. An indicator of such thought is given ably by Grover Hartman, a United Methodist layman who is executive secretary of the Indiana Council of Churches: "The mention of ecumenical in the tear sheet leads me to note that the alternatives posed do not seem to be complete. Besides organic mergers and functional denominational coalitions like JSAC, you certainly have the conciliar alterna-

135

tive in which denominations, while maintaining identity, relate closely to others on an 'inclusive,' not 'limited coalitional' basis, for exchange of views and experience, planning, witness, service, and action. I hope that you do not leave out the route of modification of conciliar structures to assure flexibility and immediacy of response. I see this as probably the most effective, least selfish, and, potentially, most valuable approach."

I can only conclude from all response that "further organic church union" is a dead horse in United Methodist thinking. Other ecumenical dimensions seem to be aborning.

Frothing from on High

"National church pronouncements are becoming counter-productive. It used to be that pronouncements and resolutions stimulated thought by calling attention to matters of concern. Now members have had their attention called to the issues long since by the newspapers and television. Many have already, therefore, formulated their opinions. For that reason, when a board precipitously makes a pronouncement, and the newspapers circulate it as a position of the church, antagonisms are aroused. 'Who says so?' members ask. 'The General Conference isn't meeting, is it?' they inquire. We had better find ways of wider involvement in formulating pronouncements or cut them out entirely—probably the latter." This comment from a South Central Program Council staff is typical of most feeling. Here seems to lie another dead horse.

The negative attitude toward national pronouncements and resolutions has come through in comments on other subjects scattered throughout this book. Most people don't want any more! Great numbers speak out spontaneously against them; not one is enthusiastically in favor. Some feel that local pronouncements, resulting from discussion nearer the grass roots, may be all right, but they are not excited about the possibilities even at that level.

Most highly irritating to respondents seem to be pronounce-ments, positions, or resolutions from "hired hands," the national staff. "The real question is not whether the church should speak out as much as it is *who* in the church should speak out, and *what* should be said. . . . Quite often some employee of an agency, who holds a position of responsibility, speaks to some issue and it is interpreted by the news media as an official position of The United Methodist Church. Local members believe the report that an official position has been taken. Staff may be well-meaning. We hope so. But they should be reminded that they do not speak for the church. When they attempt to, they raise hackles all over the conferences—especially with General Conference delegates who have voted themselves for some staff-suggested resolutions that they did not clearly understand and which were rammed through at the last minute."

A large number of respondents see resolutions and pronouncements as "insincere diversions." Indicative of that attitude is a comment from a young adult discussion group in North Central, which observes: "The United Methodist Church has fallen into the pit of 'resolutionitis' in recent years. Often a resolution is passed or a pronouncement made, in the closing hours of a session when resolutions are most often presented, with no intention of much happening as a result. So little happens, in fact, that we are led to believe that 'continuing business as usual' was intended. Some have concluded, in fact, that the procedure was just to get some confrontation group off our back. Let the church reduce her proclamations and her resolutions and *do* more! Spend more time in revising priorities than in devising insincere diversions. That will speak more loudly than words about how sincere we are." Many similar observations were made.

Comments by the hundreds came in with one clipping attached, an article entitled "Let's Have One More Moratorium —On General Board Pronouncements," by the Rev. Donald Haynes, United Methodist clergyman in Franklin, North Carolina. The article first appeared in the *North Carolina Christian Advocate*, was reprinted in the *Texas Methodist*, and heaven only knows where else. We are tempted to conclude in the Dayton office of the general Program Council that it appeared everywhere. It came to us from all points of the compass. We would feel obligated, therefore, to print the article in its entirety except for the fact that it consumes forty-seven column inches of space. With apologies to all who so enthusiastically submitted it as speaking for them, we note only Mr. Haynes's main points:

1. "Pronouncements have a 'Thus saith the Lord' connotation which implies a moral and ethical superiority" on the part of those who make them. All great prophets who made such proclamations in the past "sat where their people sat" before they spoke, a discipline in which denominational proclaimers have not engaged.

2. "Pronouncements and resolutions preempt the right of 'Little People.' . . . Nobody can assume the prerogatives of the individual Christian." The Reformation reminds us that when this has happened in the church, "cleavage and defection, separation and splintering" have resulted.

3. "The rhetorical gimmick of 'we do not speak for The United Methodist Church' is of little solace." Why then speak from an official United Methodist platform? "When a telegram goes out from a board of our church in official session, it carries the undeniable implication of speaking for the church.

4. "Pronouncements misappropriate and abort many energies of the church." Among other things, "the effective ministry of the entire church is eroded by the necessary efforts to translate, to explain, and sometimes to offset the statements of general boards, councils, etc. Local church leadership is put on the defensive.

5. "Pronouncements tend to reflect fads, opinions, and emotions as much as they do historical and theological foundations of the Christian faith. There is no wisdom inherent in numbers. Just because a 'majority present and voting' feel a certain conviction at a momentary juncture in history, we cannot assume that this is a wise position that will stand the test of time." Some of the executives who proclaim a resolution as that of "majority present and voting" are the first to question the

validity of a majority consensus from local churches on any subject.

6. "The voice of the people of God in any local community is muted by the periodic frothing from on high. Now we are met with adamant opposition and predetermined prejudice. The local pastor is weakened because he is associated with an ecclesiastical diatribe.

7. "Let there be one more moratorium—a moratorium on pronouncements and resolutions!"

There it is! The reader may wish to debate with Mr. Haynes, but if so, he will be taking on most of the respondents in this sample. They loudly applaud his views.

To United Methodists who participated, national church pronouncements and resolutions are a dead horse that will take those who have ridden it no farther.

The Lackluster Gray Vocabulary

As one reads the comments coming from United Methodists throughout the country, the impression gradually builds that the people have many hang-ups with some of the old vocabulary of the Christian faith. Most often voiced as the reason is "that the church has so profaned words by professing and teaching one thing while practicing another that the words have come to be nice talk with no one taking them seriously."

A few typical comments show the feelings. "It will most likely be easier to put meaning, which is what really matters, into new words than to attempt to resurrect the old. The quip about the difficulty of resurrecting a corpse applies here. No one has found successful the putting of new wine into old wineskins. Let's discard hypocrisy-worn vocabulary that we preach without practicing, and seek words with meaning that we are willing to live and demonstrate!" So plead a large group of young adults at a summer convocation. Numerous respondents reflect similar feelings.

The word *evangelism* is part of the dead vocabulary, as we have seen earlier. "Evangelism is a word that turns us off."

"We have used evangelism to mean so many different things, from week-long revival to bar rap sessions, that the word only means to a person what that person wants it to mean." These participants want to speak of "commitment" in the place of evangelism. That seems to be a word aborning.

A youth group states: "Evangelism turns us off, because we hear it spoken of as 'saving a person *from* this sinful world.' Such evangelism seems designed to save a person *for* a pious, innocuous fellowship preparing for life 'out there somewhere.' Commitment is a word that turns us on. Needed in the church is commitment *to* God which changes one's relationship with persons to one of love and concern and thus results in commitment to this life. The evangelistic approach doesn't make any difference, that we can see, in the way 'Christians' treat people. That jejune concept grabs nobody. The word 'commitment' has more of the jolt of Jesus in it."

The word *stewardship* is another one that no longer carries a vital meaning. Again we find that the word has been used in so many different contexts that it has become everything, yet church members "are not quite certain what." A group from a large urban church, in rejecting the idea of treating environment as a matter of stewardship, comments: "When we talk about stewardship of something, we always seem to end up talking about money. Our members are getting suspicious that talk of the 'stewardship' of the environment, or of anything else, is just a sneaky way to get around to hitting them for another buck or two. Many indicate that when they hear 'stewardship' they turn off the speech." Another similar comment goes on, "The one who cries 'stewardship' is often the poorest example of a good steward. We hear so much of 'do as I say, not as I do' that the word 'stewardship' gets weaker and weaker."

The word *mission*, too, comes in for its share of dislike. Feeling is best summed up by an executive of United Methodism's Board of Missions, Harry Haines, who states: "There is danger that when everything becomes mission, nothing is mission." Similar dismay is indicated in the comments of many that this word in the Christian vocabulary is becoming lack-luster gray—"overall blah," as one person puts it.

The word *temperance* also comes in for numerous licks—not so much because people no longer believe in the basic concept, but for two other reasons. For one thing, many react as does this young adult group from Southeastern in saying: "Temperance is another hypocritical area where words and practice do not jibe. The church continues to give lip service to a concept while not paying much serious attention to it. Members do not sense that church leadership wants to be too energetic in speaking about it. Besides, ministers take so many positions on the subject, and there are such a variety of inter-pretations of it in our literature, that everyone is confused. Also, it gets rather humorous at times to hear the wine of the Bible explained away as not really being wine by the same per-sons, laity and clergy, who insist on literalism with other Bible verses."

The other objection is stated more forcefully. A large group of ministers in North Central and a university student group in South Central, for instance, use almost the same words when they say: "There are more urgent matters demanding the con-cern of the church today than a sip of wine. We have too many church members who get very disturbed about alcohol who will not pay their workers living wages, who see no reason for talking about justice and human rights as Christian concerns, and who do not show compassion or love for people who are suffering in their own backyards."

Regardless of what we believe about temperance, it is ob-vious that there has been a gradual change in approach to it in the denomination. One typical Methodist minister says: "In my judgment the issue began to die right after World War II. This is seen in the shift in the official name of the organization which deals with the issue. Until 1960, it was the Board of Temperance. From 1960 to 1964, it was the Division of Tem-perance and General Welfare of the Board of Christian Social Concerns. Then, until 1968, the division name was changed to the Division of Alcohol Problems and General Welfare. After that date, the division is simply called the Division of General Welfare." This indicates to him and to many that interest in temperance has been declining for some time.

So we can see that large numbers of participants in the sample are reflecting against a dead-horse vocabulary in the Christian religion. They are asking for live vocabulary, with clear meaning, consistent with practice. Most are sick and tired of innocuous discussions of less important matters while talkers avoid urgent human problems about them. "We seem to want to argue about smoking or miniskirts or long hair while showing no concern for starving, suffering, exploited people about us. No wonder that our youth are sickened by the society that we are willing to them," says a group of teachers.

Bureaucratic Manipulation

Packaged programs are even now meeting with little response. Unless there is participation in the design of program, most are saying, there will be increasingly less response and implementation. "Not even whipcracking will stuff packaged programs down members' throats any longer," reflects a district superintendent. So do many more.

Bureaucratic manipulation, you will recall, is called the worst remaining paternalism in the church. Many see leaders as more willing to grant "self-determination" to overseas churches and to minority groups than to local churches. New leadership style is called for. Such a new style seems to be aborning, as we shall see in a moment.

Colts Aborning

Innovative ideas and new approaches are aborning in The United Methodist Church. Spontaneous comments reveal members' concerns on which they are "rarin' to go." Far and wide, respondents want action *now*—on curriculum and study patterns, on the youth culture, on better preaching, on the cumbersome workings of denominational structure. Just what are people saying?

New Educational Patterns

The pluralism of the day demands that the church recognize, and make authentic, differing viewpoints and different approaches, respondents declare. It is no longer easy to get consensus in the church. It is also unnecessary. No single viewpoint or approach to study and worship meets the needs of everyone in any congregation. Many approaches are needed and *must* be tried.

"Where Methodists most urgently need to break out of their one-mold complex is in the church school. Either by intent or by bungling practice we have settled into one. A wider variety of literature should be available—especially of wider theological approach. When those at study come constantly upon theological statements with which they personally, and often corporately, disagree, they get sidetracked and miss the main lesson. The sharp drop in orders for our literature speaks clearly—it must be unwanted or of no use. A wider variety of literature must be available and a wider variety of learning experiences offered. Continue the old Sunday school classes (calling them church school classes hasn't changed anything) as long as they draw interest. But make authentic in every congregation study in other ways, at other times, at other places. Temporary seminars, weeknight classes, home study groups, coffee house groups—the sky should be the limit. Pluralism must be planned for rather than resisted. People now feel free to express differences openly and to live those differences. . . . Accept them as authentic. Stop the love-us-or-leave-us attitude." In this comment from a North Central ministerial group, we catch a note sounded by many. One literature does not suffice. One study approach does not meet needs. "Let's get busy on better curriculum and educational patterns" is the cry.

The observation that much of the present curriculum material is either "unwanted or unusable" is the most generally voiced opinion. A statement from an annual conference summary in South Central, an annual conference that has engaged in widespread data gathering including twenty-eight hearings in local churches, is indicative: "There is a growing criticism of the United Methodist church school curriculum. There are certainly many who invest themselves in it and find it meaningful. However, there are two sides to the criticism. There is the criticism of content. Also, there is the criticism that even though the content is appropriate, most persons are not trained to use it effectively. In other words, either the content is not acceptable or it is not usable." Another annual conference group, this time from North Central, says: "We find that the curriculum is not being used for two reasons. The largest expression is that content needs improvement—more biblical and less socially oriented. The next most prevalent comment is that the content is the best that we have ever had but we have failed, through leadership development, to stimulate leaders and teachers to make good use of it. There seems to be an erroneous assumption behind the material that teachers are capable of using the curriculum and that they will commit the necessary preparation time to its use. We find little enthusiasm for the curriculum. We find much enthusiasm for study." Such observations are general. From everywhere they are coupled with an urging to "Go!"

A district Program Council in Michigan points up the general feeling of urgency about developing new study patterns: "Christian education is a necessity for a forward-looking church. However, the old 'Sunday school' format is out-of-date and, in fact, dying. Christian education needs to use new and up-to-date forms, the latest techniques. Students exposed to new techniques in secular education will no longer accept archaic techniques at church school. Education is becoming less and less a matter of getting something from a printed page into a student's 'information well.' The church must look immediately at the better techniques, times, and settings for the Christian education process."

The reader has been struck by now, I am certain, with how often "urgency," "immediately," and "at once" appear in the comments about Christian education. Some changes in curriculum and educational process are aborning and rarin' to go.

The Now Generation

One annual conference cries, "All indications are that youth and the church are in crisis. We had better seek solutions, and fast!" The cry is almost lost in the wild, frenzied crescendo from other groups. In many ways, this is a bronco that refuses to be ridden!

Everywhere there appears concern "about" youth, concern "of" youth, and a clash of culture with counter-culture that rattles the stained glass of cozy sanctuaries. Emerging new life styles of youth have churchmen and churchwomen scurrying around in a way once reserved in ecclesiastical fiction for church mice.

Adults are agreed about one thing in reflecting on the youth of the day—"Do something! Somebody do something!" The Northeastern annual conference summary containing that statement adds wryly, "No agreement is noted on what." Some adults urge that The United Methodist Church redouble its efforts to design attractive ministries "for" youth. A firm minority of adults advocate "less coddling and firmer discipline. 'Bring up a child in the way he should go, and when he is old he will not depart from it.'" Their attitude is similar to that of a Don Rickles joke. "About the generation gap: I say this: Talk to your kid, see what's bugging him, give his fears and desires a sympathetic airing; then take him into the cellar and work him over with the garden hose and I'm sure he'll come around." Some hang on to such a belief that youth can be whipped into line.

A much larger group of adults, however, urge that youth be allowed to design program for themselves and to help design program for the entire denomination. "In many ways," says one such group, "youth are more knowledgeable and mature in judgment than we. That's what bugs us!"

Comments from youth, and there are many, indicate that they no longer want anyone designing programs "for" them.

145

"We do not want to be treated separately in the church. We want to be treated as part of the whole program of the whole church, and we want to be involved in planning for the whole," comments a high school youth group.

Youth are "fed up" with hypocrisy, preoccupation with money and buildings, neglect of persons, and "institutionalized, insincere piosity"—among other things. One youth of Southern Illinois writes, "The average church stands as a perfect symbol of nearly everything I despise—false gentility, empty sentiment, emotional impoverishment, intellectual mediocrity, and spiritual tepidity. All churches I have visited strike me as being about as enervating as a cup of lukewarm Postum."

Adults who find youth often more knowledgeable than their elders are supported by Richard Farson in an article, "How Could Anything That Feels So Bad Be So Good?" He says: "Society may also be experiencing a reverse transmission of culture. To put it simply, today's young people probably know more than their elders. Wisdom and culture have always been transmitted from the older generation to the younger. Now, perhaps for the first time in history, there is a reversal of that process. Young people used to want to be like their elders; today it's the other way around. . . . Margaret Mead describes the plight of the over-thirty generation as being similar to that of the alien trying to learn about a foreign culture. It is a small wonder, then, that the institutions in which leadership is entrusted only to the elders (and what institution isn't?) are so unstable." [1]

The expressions from youth fall naturally together in a poem many of them sent in. It appeared in *Share*, a United Methodist youth publication.

> Hey, you!
> Look at me!
> Listen to me!
> Do you really see or hear?
> Sometimes the sound is silence

[1] *Saturday Review*, September 6, 1969, p. 20.

And the look is separateness.
I want to communicate, but don't
Know how to reach out.
So I may slap, hit, or retort
With a dirty word.
I'm really trying to say . . .
"Could you like, accept me?"
Can I trust you?
It's a risky business,
This reaching out, because
I may get hurt,
And I am afraid of that . . .
I guess I am afraid of you, too.
But somehow I need you.
And just maybe,
You could need me?

Hey, you!
Can you hear me?
I am just trying to find . . . me.
Do you have time to reach out?
To listen?
To help me see . . .
and be . . . *me!*"

In that is the whinny of a colt aborning! United Methodists seem certain of one thing: the church must respond! As James Nettleton, a program director in Southern Illinois, says: "We must not sit complacently by thinking that someday youth will grow up, become like us and become active in the church as we know it. Neither will getting a new pastor who can 'reach the youth' be the answer. This is a call to the church to reexamine thoroughly its life and practices." Youth are ready to be a part of doing just that. "Right on!"

Pulpit Power

Spontaneously, most of the laity in this sample tell us there is another colt aborning—demands for good preaching. "Whoever started the rumor that preaching is no longer effective or wanted?" asks a large group of laity from the southeast. "Must have been some preachers too lazy to work on sermons—we've

147

heard some of their sermons. The rumor was not from us. Our members still believe that good preaching gets more response than anything else. Of course, many of the somniferous lecturettes that we hear move nobody! Good preaching could! How about a renewed emphasis on inspired, enthusiastic preaching?"

A young minister of Batesville, Indiana, the Rev. Allan Wilson, confesses to impoverishment in clerical thought when he says, "Ministers of the gospel have the most important thing in the world to proclaim. Yet nobody on earth talks about more unimportant things than preachers. I may be betraying one of the top secrets of the brotherhood, but when preachers get together, they don't always talk about the things that matter. Not much is said about the way God is working in our world today. Little is mentioned about the needs of people in our parishes. We talk about church buildings, and about who's going to what church next June, and about how we are not appreciated for the hard work we do. Lots of talking—but the word that saves is usually missing." Many laymen say it is missing in preaching, too.

Clear calls for good preaching are heard, largely from laity, in many hearings in the annual conferences. "Thirty hearings in our annual conference lead us to revise our feelings about the relevancy of preaching! People are pleading for good preaching in all situations. Our people are agreed that they want good preaching, that they fight to keep preachers who can preach, that the preaching hour still gets more commitment to important issues than all bureaucratic pronouncements and print."

Many district superintendents perceive wide demands for "good preachers." "The most asked question of our cabinet at appointment time is, 'Can he preach?' We wish that we could more often answer, Yes!" A South Central district superintendent says: "One of my churches raised their preacher's salary three thousand dollars for next year. When I got a little curious about such a large raise, the lay leader said, 'We couldn't afford not to. He can preach and people pack the place to hear. He is the first good preacher that we have had, and we hope to keep him. Our plan is to raise his salary so fast that you can't move him!' "

Franklin Littell, in *Sermons to Intellectuals,* observes: "The sermon is now regarded as a debased form of currency. . . . Yet there was a time when the sermon was a major literary form, and there were generations when the Protestant clergy . . . proclaimed a message which shaped the affairs of men and nations. . . . Great preaching is preaching for a verdict." The laity strongly urge a return to such preaching. Are they but reminiscing? They don't think so!

Tune Up

"The way in which we conduct the work of The United Methodist Church is more in need of attention than is structure," says an annual conference group in the southeast. A similar group from North Central concurs: "We have found that 'restructuring' in our annual conference hasn't changed much of anything. Under new organizational committees and task forces, we continue to operate with little openness, little flexibility, and much paternalism. We are more in need of changing our style of operating than the machinery of the organization. Our new structure concentrates decision-making in the hands of fewer persons than before—the opposite of what is needed." A ground swell of expression fom United Methodists is not for change of structure as much as it is for a new style of operation, whatever the structure. A colt seems aborning!

The dimensions of what United Methodists want in a new style of operation can be seen emerging throughout the data. The buds burst forth at many places.

Opportunities for more participation are urgently requested. Laity seek more participation in decision-making, including the use of funds; clergy recognize the quest as valid. Minority groups demand participation in decisions and programs that affect their destiny. Youth and younger adults request authentic recognition for their participation. All respondents feel that

149

the participation of the average church member is as important as the participation of church leadership. Pluralism seems to demand that people with differing ideological and theological views be co-participants. "United Methodists must learn from each other and learn to work *together*."

It is often true that participants more accurately reflect the needs of an organization than can anyone else. The story is told of one of the nation's atomic generating plants for electrical power. Because it was a relatively untried power source, unusual care was taken to build in safety devices. No one knew just what to expect. And, as was expected, many bugs developed. Worst was that the generator only ran sporadically. It would start up and suddenly shut down, run like a watch for a while and, seemingly for no reason at all, stop. Technicians went over the controls and found them in perfect working order. Baffled, they called in an expert to study the matter. He, too, was baffled. One day he ran into one of the building custodians who asked, "Say, if you're an expert on these things, can you tell me one thing? Why is it that every time somebody in the upstairs office flushes the john this whole plant shuts down?" There was the answer. Each time someone flushed the john, the water pressure dropped and an automatic water pressure control shut down the generating plant. Sometimes you find out more about what's wrong by involving someone on the work force than by calling in an expert.

United Methodists are calling for a more cooperative style of operation. Respondents indicate that the extensiveness of need, the limitation of available resources, and ecumenical mandates combine to require cooperation throughout and across the units of the denomination, and between the denomination and groups with common interests in the community. Many speak of strong disappointment that "while our executives debate whether coordination, cooperation, or correlation is more desirable, the real noncooperative stance of agencies is revealed. Too often they still go their selfish, unilateral ways!"

More innovation, and the flexibility that allows and supports it, are necessary. Innovative ideas should be welcomed in the church. Old approaches should be constantly evaluated, in the light of Christian purpose, to discover whether they are based more on culture and custom than on Christian mission. New models should also be tried and their validity examined. The life styles, worship patterns, and service commitments of youth may bring new vitality to the church.

Communication that is swift, communication that is clear, and communication that goes two ways is called for. Comments indicate a widespread conviction that messages have been getting through from national leadership to the local church, although too slowly, but that messages have not been getting through from the local church back. "At least," says one North Central annual conference summary, "there was no indication that any message was being heard by the national leaders until money tightened up. That seems to be one local churchogram that clears the wires. It would be better to keep them clear."

Finally, a style of operation that includes strategic planning and action is requested. If the denomination is to move ahead with relevancy in the complex issues and needs of the day, most feel that thoughtful planning and risk-taking action are necessities. These must be based on careful attention to Christian purpose. "What are we in business for?" is a basic question. With that in mind, wide participation must be sought in determining needed mission and appropriate action. Above all, the result must not be a package of "everyone doing the same thing at the same time in the same way." More choice must be stimulated on the part of the local churches, who must be challenged to move out with action that is relevant "in their place."

10

TEMPTED, YET COMPELLED!

> But innovation is more than a new method. It is a new
> view of the universe, as one of risk rather than of
> chance or of certainty. It is a new view of man's role
> in the universe; he creates order by taking risks. And
> this means that innovation, rather than being an as-
> sertion of human power, is an acceptance of human
> responsibility.
>
> —Peter Drucker, *Landmarks of Tomorrow*

Not all United Methodists believe the church can move on.
Predictably enough, there are those among the respondents
who want to abandon ship. They see the church as incapable
or incompetent in the contemporary situation. "The church,"
says one group, "is so much a part of the problem that she cannot be part of the solution." They are about to desert.

That kind of response in tense times is nothing new. "Fears
do make us traitors," Shakespeare once wrote. The fearful are
always present! "There is scarcely anything around us but ruin
and despair," cried William Pitt in the eighteenth century. As
the next opened, Wilberforce observed, "I dare not marry, the
future is so dark and unsettled." About fifty years later the
Duke of Wellington, on the even of his death, thanked God
that he would "be spared from seeing the consummation of
ruin that is gathering about us."

So we might go on until the day this paragraph is written.
In the morning mail I received another response from a woman
in Indiana. Her comments are perceptive and keen, tempered

by years of service in the church. On the final page, in the neat style of a calligrapher, she writes: "I'm very confused by all that is happening, and very frightened—and very tired. I guess it's time for me to quit." But she won't. Her other comments confess to an inner compulsion that allows no "juniper treeitis," that calls her instead to involvement. So did most respondents. Tempted to quit, yet compelled to go on!

Thousands of United Methodists shout their belief that "the church ain't done yet!" Most are not about to give up. Sensitivity and growing commitment show clearly in the comments submitted. So much openness and flexibility are expressed that I am led to believe in the possibility of relevant Christian involvement in living—a conclusion that has been hard to reach amid the churchy concerns of recent years.

One cause for optimism is that a majority of the host who responded accept change as normal. They ask that beliefs, values, and practices be reevaluated and more clearly formulated in the light of rapid change.

Those who do not believe that change is normal should look at their high school yearbook. The buildings pictured, the styles worn, the faces once familiar—all have changed in a few short years. "Permanency exists only in the uninterrupted continuity of change," as E. A. Gutkind observes.

The data show that change is being accepted as a continuing and accelerating force in the world. Respondents are facing the fact that change is a mandate upon all humanity to be more flexible and innovative. "Old ways won't wash much longer. We'll need faster drip-dry approaches," says a local church leadership group.

Of course, we are threatened by change. Most of us, when we are candid, confess to nostalgic longing for a simple, quiet, unperturbed local church. We are awakening, however, to the fact that such a church does not exist—and it would be terrible if it did! To find a quiet congregation would be to find one unaware, uninvolved, and un-Christlike! Acceptance of this fact in the data is encouraging.

Written comments show a readiness to move out deliberately

to meet change. Crisis reaction is no longer regarded as a valid way of operation. Many agree with Alexander Pope, who said,

> Be not the first by whom the new is tried;
> Nor yet the last to lay the old aside.

Of course, a few would accept newness without thinking just because it is new—they want to be first. A few more would accept almost anything because of boredom or disgust with what they have. Most, however, want to plan for newness because change demands new approaches.

Respondents ask for assistance in figuring out when to hold on and when to let loose, a sign of needed flexibility. On that basis the requests for more lay participation are encouraging too. If laity are involved in discerning when new approaches are more valid than old, they will need no convincing when movement is needed.

Laity involvement will be welcomed. Church people have been bludgeoned with their evasion of responsibility and with the gospel mandate for Christian involvement in the secular world. That the message has gotten through, that willingness to respond is now evident, points to exciting possibilities.

I am encouraged, too, by the awareness on the part of most respondents that whatever concerns humanity must concern the church. The ancient, yet strangely modern, heresy of the church ministering only to the spiritual side of life is refuted. With continuing care for the souls of men, United Methodists express an awareness that the church cannot fully serve humanity without filling hungry stomachs, educating blighted minds, and restoring denied opportunities. Commitment to God and commitment to justice and humanization go together. The church must be able to say to people, "We are interested in your total life," or it has nothing to say.

So I am encouraged to find in these data a growing commitment to the concept that the church is here to serve the world and not herself. Most respondents see that the church has been too closely tethered to sacred buildings, sacred prac-

154

tices, and sacred times. They are keenly aware that Christians must come out from behind their stained glass and *be* Christians, in the home, in business, in secular life, and in relationships with all persons.

In *Only One Way Left*, George MacLeod expresses this feeling when he says: "Jesus Christ was not crucified in a cathedral between two candles, but on a cross between two thieves; on the town garbage heap; on a crossroads so cosmopolitan that they had to write his title in Hebrew and Latin and Greek; at the kind of place where cynics talk smut, and thieves curse, and soldiers gamble. Because this is where he died and that is what he died about. And that is where churchmen should be and that is what churchmen should be about."

And So!

Those responsible for planning in United Methodism's general agencies, working with laity and clergy across the nation, are using these data in discussing priorities for denominational programming. Seven emerging priorities are seen at this time in the light of Christian purpose:

1. Commitment, nurture, and renewal
2. A better style of denominational operation
3. Theological reflection and witness
4. Concerns for persons
5. Concerns for justice and development
6. Cultural concerns
7. Human survival concerns

No attempt is being made right now to develop these priorities in final detail. Planning process, by its very nature, leaves the final development to planning groups at all levels as they struggle with demands for Christian mission in their own place. The analysis of these data will be but one input in their planning.

As planning and development of strategies proceeds for January 1, 1973, and beyond, priorities will be brought into clearer focus, and others added. The denominational Program Council suggests some reasons for looking at the priorities named.

1. Commitment, nurture, and renewal are basic to all priorities. More comments were received on this general subject than on any other. Commitment to God through Jesus Christ, resulting in commitment to serve humanity, is vital. Needs for the future include a definition of the Christian faith that conserves the meaning of historic tenets and creeds yet speaks to people of the space age, an understanding of the meaning of commitment to the God of that faith, continuing nurture (education) that will enable clergy and laity together to engage in renewal of the church and ministry to the world, and membership training that leads to understanding and action on these concepts.

2. The need for a better style of denominational organization was fully discussed in chapter 9. Therefore, the elements of that style are only listed here: participation, cooperation, innovation, clear communication, and strategic planning with action.

3. In theological reflection and witness we will give thought to the way in which we formulate our theology, to the content of our theology, and to the contemporary ways we communicate our beliefs. Let's call those three dimensions style, symbol, and witness.

The aim of style should be to assist the church to develop theology while living our beliefs, not to produce an abstract statement of intellectual truth, important as clarity in the church's theology may be. In part theology will be formulated on the firing line, with clergy and laity in dialogue with each other and with those whom they serve. Christian theology will be the work of the entire church, requiring that seminaries, clergy, and laity become involved together in relating the church's historic faith and contemporary engagement in mission in such a way that each aids in the interpretation and understanding of the other.

A theological symbol can be a word, a sign, a color, a dance, or a song—among other things. The aim of symbol will be to

156

present biblical truth in a way intelligible to contemporary man. It will look theologically at present-day experiences to find those matters in human experience which can be explained better through Christian faith than through secular understanding. If new symbols better communicate the historic faith, we shall use them. Change and the future will be viewed as arenas of possibility rather than unrelieved threat. The demands of individuals for self-determination will be seen as potential ground for justice, not chaos. Secularization and pluralism of views and practice will be approached with openness, hope, and confidence.

The aim of witness is communication. The church's understanding of the faith will be sharpened so that it can be clearly communicated to others. We shall "testify" by living and speaking to that which we believe. We shall develop sensitive listening to persons not claiming Christian faith. Especially, we shall attempt to engage in conversation with others in matters of everyday life where faith is called for. Christian faith will be seen as a basic attitude, not just a system of creeds and doctrines. Greater consistency will be sought between the way we live and our professed beliefs.

4. The priority of concern for persons recognizes that Jesus taught that each individual has supreme worth in the sight of God. The people called Christian have fallen far short of assisting people in finding their full humanity, a basic Christian responsibility. People will be freed to develop their God-given talents and capacities for creative living. They will be enabled to grow in their acceptance and understanding of others. Action will be taken to change society's cruelty systems, in many of which the people called Christian have unwittingly participated.

5. The priority of justice and development recognizes that the church too often has stopped by taking some old clothes and a basket of food to the poor family down the block without going on to help change the systems that have caused the poverty. Jesus demonstrated in his teaching and action that direct service to alleviate the suffering of individuals is not

157

enough. Justice must be sought for all. Racial and cultural groups must be empowered to achieve their own cultural goals. Equality and empowerment for minority groups must be sought. Repression in society must be confronted.

6. The priority of cultural concerns seeks greater understanding of the benefits of intercultural mixing while maintaining cultural identities. One lowest-common-denominator culture is no answer. The church will deal with the fear, shock, and frustration associated with rapid change and clashing cultural patterns by deliberately taking part in managing change.

7. Human survival is given priority because we live in a time of possible total extinction of the human race. In that context our youth turn to a "now" style of living. War, abuse of the environment, exploding population, atomic weapons, possible genetic and chemical control of individuals are among the factors that contribute to a feeling of threat and demand the attention of committed Christians. We shall attempt to help people understand that concern for human survival is a necessary part of a view of the universe as God's creation and thus an object of his, and our, loving care. The church will be involved in matters of war and peace, responsible use and restoration of the environment, and rethinking value systems on which decisions are made about biomedical practices.

Right On!

The Chinese have an old saying that there are five points to the compass—the place where you stand and four directions. Before we move out to do anything, they say, we must first of all find where we are. That is the most important point.

These data, and their analysis, help show United Methodism where it stands. Continuing examination of the response in the light of Christian purpose will help church people, clergy and laity together, discover what they should be doing and where they should be going.